PICK AND PLAN

PICK AND PLAN

100

BRAIN-COMPATIBLE
STRATEGIES FOR LESSON DESIGN

BRENDA UTTER

CORWIN PRESS
A SAGE Publications Company
Thousand Oaks, CA 91320

For information:

Corwin Press
A Sage Publications Company
2455 Teller Road
Thousand Oaks, California 91320
www.corwinpress.com

Sage Publications Ltd.
1 Oliver's Yard
55 City Road
London EC1Y 1SP
United Kingdom

Sage Publications India Pvt. Ltd.
B 1/I 1 Mohan Cooperative
    Industrial Area
Mathura Road, New Delhi 110 044
India

Sage Publications Asia-Pacific Pte. Ltd.
33 Pekin Street #02-01
Far East Square
Singapore 048763

Printed in the United States of America.

Library of Congress Cataloging-in-Publication Data

Utter, Brenda.
Pick and plan : 100 brain-compatible strategies for lesson design / Brenda Utter.
    p. cm.
Includes bibliographical references and index.
ISBN 978-1-4129-5113-5 (cloth) — ISBN 978-1-4129-5114-2 (pbk.)
    1. Lesson planning. 2. Learning. 3. Teaching. I. Title. II. Title: 100 brain-compatible strategies for lesson design.

LB1027.4.U88 2007
371.3′028—dc22

2006101257

This book is printed on acid-free paper.

07   08   09   10   11   10   9   8   7   6   5   4   3   2   1

Acquisitions Editor:	Faye Zucker
Editorial Assistant:	Gem Rabanera
Production Editor:	Sarah K. Quesenberry
Copy Editor:	Edward Meidenbauer
Typesetter:	C&M Digitals (P) Ltd.
Proofreader:	Caryne Brown
Indexer:	Kathy Paparchontis
Cover Designer:	Lisa Miller

Contents

Acknowledgments

Nobody really does anything alone, and many people have helped me in my educational journey. I've always had the foundation of a great family and supportive friends. I was further blessed by being hired by Dave McGuire, who showed me what a true professional in education looked like. I work for a wonderful and progressive school system, Warsaw Community Schools, where I have been encouraged to continually learn, grow, and try new things. Eventually, my passage into professional development led me to find a friend and mentor, Lynne Ames. Lynne not only taught me the ropes of professional development; she has also served as a sounding board throughout the whole learning process. Finally, I have always had a terrific staff and great students, all of whom have served as guinea pigs and willing vessels as I tried out the strategies in this book. Without them, this book would not have happened.

About the Author

Brenda Utter is a teacher and the program coordinator of Warsaw Adult Education, located in Warsaw, Indiana. She has been working in education for more than 12 years, and her experiences include teaching third grade, high school Spanish, and remedial reading, as well as adult education. She spent more than 13 years working in the industrial sector and has created and taught English as a second language programs for workplace literacy. Brenda has also been involved in professional development for the past 7 years and has conducted trainings in several states.

Brenda earned a Bachelor of Arts degree from Ball State University, with majors in Economics and Marketing and minors in Spanish and International Business. She also has a Master of Science degree in Language Education from Indiana University in Bloomington, Indiana. She holds a teaching license in Elementary Education with a minor in Reading from Indiana University in South Bend, Indiana, and is currently working on her administrator's licensure from Indiana Wesleyan University.

Part I
At the Beginning

You might be asking yourself if you really need to read this part or if you can just skip it and get on to the lesson planning. There are very good reasons to have some basic knowledge about how the brain works if you are going to be teaching. First, you should know how learning actually takes place in the brain if you are going to make physical changes in the brain, and when you learn something you are making a physical change in the brain. You should also understand the things that enhance or inhibit learning. The Hippocratic Oath for physicians includes the phrase, "I will do no harm . . ." I believe the same should be the case for teachers. Making a good lesson plan begins with understanding the students. One step toward understanding the students is learning to understand how the brain processes new information.

1

The Building Blocks of the Brain

How We Learn

Educational trends are cyclical. When I was in the first grade learning to read, everything was whole language. I never learned phonics. Many years later, I was substitute teaching in the first grade, and the children were doing a phonics lesson. I did not know how to do it, and the 6-year-olds did. They had to teach me. Shortly after that incident, I returned to college to work on a second bachelor's degree. This degree was in elementary education with a reading minor. Again, the cycle was taking a whole language focus. I still did not learn phonics. However, in the practice of teaching I found that many people, especially those with reading problems, truly need phonics and phonemic awareness training (which is something I had never even heard of when I got my degree in reading). So why is it that professional educators appear to be incapable of deciding what is really the best way to teach something, even something as important as reading? I believe there are two major reasons for this.

The first reason is that educators have historically tried to fit all children into the same mold. Howard Gardner has shown us in his book *Frames of Mind: The Theory of Multiple Intelligences* (1983) that we all have different innate talents and ways in which we learn best. No two brains are exactly alike, which means that no two people are going to learn in exactly the same way. You cannot fit human beings into a mold, however convenient that might be.

The second reason for the cyclical trends in education is that we were treating symptoms, not the underlying problem. Think of a doctor trying to treat someone for high blood pressure before the blood pressure cuff was invented. He may have told the patient to relax and get more rest, but he could not have said why that would work, or even be sure that it would work. He just knew that for many of his patients rest and relaxation seemed to fix the problem. The very same thing has been happening in education. We could tell you that for many people, surrounding them with language was all they needed in order to learn to read. Then we noticed those for whom that didn't work, and decided to apply to all the children the "cure" (phonics) that worked for that group. Soon, we noticed that many of the children didn't need the phonics but just seemed to pick up reading. Hence we have developed a cyclical nature.

Once the children reach upper-elementary and middle-school ages, it is assumed that they know how to read. It is further assumed that they have longer attention spans, which may or may not be true, and that they will be able to learn well by listening to the teacher lecture. This latter assumption is rarely true. Whereas in kindergarten and the lower elementary grades children commonly learn things by hands-on activities and with songs, as children grow into teenagers they are often expected to learn by only two modes: listening and reading. Many people don't learn well with these modes; some don't learn in these ways at all. Those who don't learn in these modes are often left behind and eventually drop out of school, frequently with the intention of getting their GEDs. Unfortunately, if they attend adult basic education classes, they often find that these classes are taught in much the same manner, and the students fail once again, probably for the last time in education.

> Briefly summarized, Howard Gardner has two sections to his multiple intelligences theory: (a) We have the ability to develop intellectual capacity, and (b) there are many ways to be smart. There is more than one human intelligence; in fact, there are multiple intelligences. Each person has all of the intelligences in a unique pattern. The Multiple Intelligences School, according to Bruce and Linda Campbell (Campbell, Campbell, & Dickinson, 2004) in *Teaching and Learning Through Multiple Intelligences,* is a place where "Teachers believe students are intellectually competent in multiple ways and communicate such beliefs to students" (p. 332).

In the past few years, however, we have been able to tap into the discoveries of brain research and find out how the brain is actually processing information and learning for all age groups. (In the previous analogy, our blood pressure cuff has been invented.) Although there are still many mysteries to be uncovered, we finally understand why some things work and others don't, and what the most efficient ways of learning are. In this book we will first look at the major operations of the brain and some of the outcomes of research, then apply this knowledge to the classroom by developing lesson plans that take advantage of these findings. In this way, we can reach all of our students with a variety of teaching methods and strategies. I hope you will find this research and its application refreshing, and maybe even life changing. I have.

■ BRAIN FUNCTIONS

The average human brain weighs about three pounds, or approximately 2% of body weight. At birth, most babies have brains that weigh around one pound; by the age of five, it will have grown to about 90% its adult size. The brain consumes

25% of the body's oxygen and 20%–30% of the body's nutrients, although it cannot store energy. The brain also uses about 70% of the body's glucose. If the brain were to be removed from the skull, it would look a bit like a large pinkish-gray walnut with a consistency akin to that of tofu. The brain can be divided into two halves, separated vertically (as though drawing a line from the chin to the nose, between the brows, and around through the top of the head). Each half is called a cerebral hemisphere. The outside layer of each hemisphere is further divided into sections, or lobes. There are four lobes to the brain. Both hemispheres contain these mirror-image lobes, although they take on slightly different jobs according to the side of the brain in which they are located. Although there are two of each lobe, one on each hemisphere, they are usually referred to in the singular. The lobes are frontal, temporal, parietal, and occipital. We will briefly look at the function of each of these lobes.

> There are several very good sources for the anatomy of the brain on-line. A couple of example of these are:
>
> www.brainconnection.com by Robert Sylwester (2005) and www.brains.org by Kathie Nunley
>
> These are user-friendly sites that make the brain research to education connections.

Think of the last time someone told you a truly funny joke. Among other functions that went on, the frontal lobe allowed you to attend to the joke long enough to hear it. It also caused you to smile or laugh, without conscious effort, at the punch line. The frontal lobe is located immediately behind the forehead and has many duties. It is the emotional control center (conscious appreciation of emotion) and home to the personality. It is the storage area for working memory, which lasts from 5 to 20 seconds. It is also involved with fine motor skills (e.g., finger dexterity), spontaneous facial expressions, problem solving, divergent thinking, flexibility, planning, initiation, impulse control, willpower, verbal expression (how much you talk), and social and sexual behavior. The very front section (or cortex) of this lobe, the prefrontal cortex, is where the personality and emotional traits are housed. It is also where the abilities to concentrate and attend can be found.

During the same joke, the temporal lobe processed the words you were hearing and allowed you to make sense of them. The temporal lobe is, not surprisingly, located around the temples. Picture a balding man with a strip of hair that runs over his ears and around the back of his head. At the very back of that strip is the occipital lobe, but at the sides are the temporal lobes. The temporal lobes also serve several functions. They are a storage area for long-term memory and process auditory input and oral language comprehension (usually only on the left side). They are also the center for some of the reading functions (e.g., decoding).

> A good source for more detail on this information is *How the Brain Learns* (3rd ed.), by David Sousa (2006).

If the joke teller was using gestures and body language while relaying the joke, you perceived these through your parietal lobe. The parietal (pa-RYE-i-tal) lobe sits at the crown of your head, like a skull cap. It deals primarily with functions connected with movement, orientation, calculation, and certain types of recognition. Mainly, it is responsible for two functions: sensation and perception, and integrating sensory input (mostly visual). The parietal lobe also helps with forming spatial relationships, including left–right distinctions.

> For a thorough explanation of vocabulary and the functions of the different parts of the brain, see Robert Sylwester's (2005) book, *How to Explain a Brain: An Educator's Handbook of Brain Terms and Cognitive Processes.*

Finally, the occipital lobe is much easier to understand because its jobs are not so broad in spectrum. The occipital lobe allowed you to see the person telling the joke. It is located at the back of the brain and is the center for visual perception. Eye movement is not controlled here, but this is where the information from the eye is sent for interpretation.

In addition to the lobes, it is necessary to know some information about another section of the brain, and about what goes on a little deeper inside the brain. First, the cerebellum is located just above the nape of the neck, toward the back and at the base of the brain, just above the brain stem. From this area come your coordination of voluntary motor movement, balance and equilibrium, and muscle tone. Your cerebellum allowed you to stand upright while hearing the joke.

On the medial surface (inside) of the temporal lobe are structures critical for normal human functioning as well as for learning. They are sometimes known as the limbic system, and they are located in the very center of the brain. In the limbic system we will briefly look at the corpus callosum, thalamus, hypothalamus, the hippocampus, and the amygdala.

The corpus callosum is located between the cortex (lobes) and the limbic system, which is beneath it. It joins the two hemispheres of the brain and acts as a bridge, or maybe a superhighway, between them. It constantly moves information back and forth between the two sides so that they can effectively act as one brain.

The thalamus relays information received from diverse brain regions to the cerebral cortex for further processing. It is involved in motor control and receives signals from every sensory system, except olfactory (smell).

Imagine that you have been busy at work for several hours. All of a sudden, you realize that you are hungry. Your hypothalamus has kicked in. The hypothalamus is hormone control central. It controls autonomic functions, emotions, endocrine functions, body temperature, and motor functions, and it regulates the cardiovascular system, food and water intake, and wake and sleep cycles. It constantly adjusts the body to keep it optimally adapted to the environment, and information from throughout the body is continually fed to it.

This brings us to the hippocampus and amygdala. The hippocampus is involved in forming and retrieving memories. It is where incoming factual information rests until it is either tagged to be sent to long-term memory or dumped (forgotten) as being unimportant. The hippocampus moves information from the working memory to a holding area. The information is then held and evaluated for hours, sometimes days. During this time, the hippocampus is searching the brain for related information. If it finds that the information is important for survival, it is further processed to long-term memory; if not, the information is discarded. Almost all learning is processed here. If the joke in the aforementioned analogy had been tagged as being important to remember, it would have been sent to another area while you were sleeping. The best way to ensure that this happens is through rehearsal and rehearsal. Repeat the joke within 10 minutes of hearing it, again after 24 hours, and again in a week.

At some time or other, most people have been in a position in which they were concentrating on something when a person came up behind them and startled them, making them jump. In this situation, you usually don't consciously think you are in danger, but the noise is unexpected. The incoming information passed through the amygdala, and a signal of danger was rapidly sent to the hypothalamus so it could prepare the body for flight, fight, or freeze. The amygdala, located at the ends of the hippocampus and shaped like an almond, is the place where information of an emotional nature is processed. If information is tagged as having emotional significance, it is then moved to another part of the brain. If you were to experience an event that made your heart race or your palms sweat, remembering it may cause these reactions to recur, as in posttraumatic stress disorder. This is the work of the amygdala.

In addition to the limbic system, as we move a little farther down we find the brain stem. The brain stem is made up of the pons, midbrain, and medulla oblongata. Together, they regulate heart rate, blood pressure, breathing, arousal, and alertness. The brain stem connects directly to the spinal cord and carries information from the body to the brain.

Knowing a bit about the operation of the brain will help as we look at different pathways memory can take. There are four different ways in which learning can happen. Learning can be semantic, episodic, procedural, or emotional. Once you understand the pathways of learning that actually occur in the brain, you can better make decisions about how you are going to teach a subject.

MEMORY PATHWAYS ■

Semantic Memory

Think of all the years you spent in school. How did you learn all of the information you now know? Chances are, most of it you learned by reading, with listening to some lectures thrown in there, too. Semantic memory is the type that is overwhelmingly the most commonly used memory pathway in schools. It is learned from such delivery systems as textbook reading; lecture; and teacher-led, whole-class discussion.

The brain was designed first and foremost for survival. Semantic memory is the least important for survival; therefore the brain is poorly designed for this form of storage and retrieval. As new information enters the brain through the brain stem, it travels through the thalamus and is sent to the hippocampus. If the incoming information is factual, the hippocampus will search for matching information. There are four implications to this:

1. This memory pathway will be greatly enhanced if the learner has accessed prior knowledge before the learning activity began.

2. Information should be processed in small chunks; the hippocampus is easily overloaded by unconnected pieces of information, so the more information is related, or "chunked" together, the more efficiently the brain can relay the information to appropriate storage systems.

3. All learning activities should be followed by processing time. If the hippocampus is overloaded, it will dump old information to make room for the new. Information is processed during downtime, when the brain is at rest. Therefore, allowing students a couple of minutes of processing time after conveying information will enhance the brain's ability to store the information.

4. Finally, rehearsal, rehearsal, rehearsal. Information must be repeated and rehearsed several times, possibly in several different ways, before long-term memory is formed. The good news about this memory pathway is that once long-term memory is formed, it is generally very stable; recalling the memory rarely changes the memory.

Teaching strategies for accessing the semantic memory pathway include the following:

- Teach students to use mnemonic devices.
- Read about the subject from a variety of sources.
- Have students write about what they have learned.
- Conduct peer discussion (not teacher-led discussion).
- Encourage peer teaching.
- Draw concept maps.
- Compare new information to old using metaphors and analogies.
- Use various questioning strategies (to stimulate thought and discussion).
- Build thematic units.
- Read and create poetry or stories.
- Think–pair–share.
- Brainstorm.

> How the learner processes new information presented in school has a great impact on the quality of what is learned and is a major factor in determining whether and how it will be retained.... Teachers with a greater understanding of the types of memory and how they form can select strategies that are likely to improve the retention and retrieval of learning.
>
> —David Sousa (2006), *How the Brain Learns (3rd ed.)*, p. 85

> In his book *Brain Compatible Strategies*, Eric Jensen (1997) states:
>
> Which is better, presenter-directed discussions or open, unguided student discussions? It depends on the topic. If the topic is academic, the younger ones (up to age ten) do better with presenter-directed. Older students do better without presenter direction. Studies suggest that the most likely way to get learner-motivated change is to allow students unguided discussion time on the topic.
> The more learners feel controlled, directed, and manipulated, the less likely they are to change their behavior. (p. 60)

Episodic Memory

> To find more information on memory pathways, see *Becoming a "Wiz" at Brain-Based Teaching*, by Marilee Sprenger (2007). She does a very good job of explaining the uses of several different aspects of brain research in the classroom.

Episodic memory is like the realty business—the three most important aspects are location, location, and location. How many times have you walked to a different room in your house, only to find when you got there that you had no idea why you went there in the first place? Oftentimes, if you return to the place where you originally got the idea, you can remember it again. This is episodic memory. If people receive information in a specific location, they will more easily remember it in the same location. This type of memory is easier to access than the semantic pathway. It is the gateway to the hippocampus; the context of learning provides additional information that is as much a part of the learning as the actual context. The drawback to using this type of learning in school is that if the students are taught in one room and tested in another, they will lose their "hook" for memory retrieval. Also, episodic memory is easily corrupted over time. Memories are not stored in one location; they are in several different lobes of the brain. Each time we retrieve memory in this way, we are actually re-creating the memory by pulling the various pieces together from differing locations. Every time this is done, small changes in the memory can be made.

When I was very small, my family lived in a huge old farmhouse that sat on the top of a hill, with a retaining wall close to the road. I was 4 years old when we moved from this house and my younger sister was 2. I very clearly remember walking along the top of the retaining wall with my sister, even though we were not supposed to be that close to the road. I also remember knowing that if we fell off this wall, we would die. Many years later I was home on a visit from college. My sister asked me if I wanted to go see the old house where we used to live. When we drove over there I was absolutely astonished. At most, that retaining wall was 18 inches high! I had always remembered it as being 4 or 5 feet high. I had talked with friends about our bravery (stupidity) as children to walk along the wall when we knew what the consequences could be. Part of the problem was one of perception: I was very small at the time, and it may have looked big to me. However, I believe that most of the problem with my story was that the wall got bigger every time I retrieved the memory. Maybe in some fish stories the fish actually *are* growing!

Teaching strategies for accessing the episodic memory pathway include the following:

- Change where the instructor stands in the classroom.
- Change where the students sit in the classroom.
- Use colors! This could be paper, chalk, markers, pens, or bulletin boards.
- Dress up and use props when teaching.
- Have the students dress up and use props.
- Use storytelling. They are visualizing being in another location.
- Have students make posters.
- Invite guest speakers.
- Use novelty to introduce a new subject.
- Take field trips.
- Do ongoing projects.

Procedural Memory

A couple of years ago I had a friend visit me from another country. She wanted to borrow my bike so that she could get around during the day while everyone else was at work; driving a car in a foreign country made her nervous. I got my bike out of the rafters in the garage and fixed it up for her. Before giving it to her, I rode it myself to make sure everything was in working order.

In *Designing Brain-Compatible Learning* by Gayle Gregory and Terence Parry (2006), the authors state:

The learning of physical skills involves the brain and the body in highly complex and integrated ways. This dual processing of information gives rise to extremely complex cognitive maps, which may be difficult to acquire, but once they are learned they are rarely forgotten.... Procedural memory has an unlimited capacity and requires only moderate intrinsic motivation. Yet hands-on experiences are often regarded as frivolous and a waste of time unsuited to academic learning in many schools. (p. 21)

It had been more than 10 years since I had been on a bicycle, but it never occurred to me that I might forget how to ride. Of course, I did not forget. I got on it and rode it around the block a couple of times before giving it to her. The reason I could ride the bike without reading instructions, reciting the steps, or using anything else to refresh my memory is that I had learned it procedurally. Procedural memory is often called muscle memory. It is the memory of movement and processes the body (mind) has learned. These would include such skills as walking, driving a car, tying a shoe, and other things we do every day without consciously thinking about all the steps involved.

Procedural memory is stored in the cerebellum once it has become routine. It is the storage of procedural memories that allows humans to do two things at once (but only one thing consciously). The best way to access procedural memory is to do what you were doing when you learned the activity in the first place. If teaching semantic information, one can take advantage of procedural memory by tying physical movement to the learning to enhance memory. It must be understood, however, that the students may need to repeat the movement to help recall the semantic information.

Teaching strategies for accessing the procedural memory pathway include:

- Dance.
- Play games that involve movement.
- Have the students stand for short lectures.
- Use role-play.
- Drama.
- Use the same process repeatedly until it becomes a habit.
- Draw the ideas.
- Use action!

Emotional Memory

If you think back to events that happened in your childhood, almost all of your memories will be hinged on emotions. Whether the emotions are anticipation, surprise, joy, sadness, trust, disgust, fear, anger, guilt, or something else, we remember emotions. The emotional pathway takes precedence over all others. Our emotions are our personalities, and they guide us through most of the decision making we do. Many of the strategies used to engage the emotional memory pathway also activate other memory storage areas. The amygdala, the center for emotional memory, not only allows us to feel love, humor, and enjoyment for the arts and music, it also helps us to have creative play and imagination and make decisions.

Some stress is necessary for learning, but both too much and too little emotion can inhibit memory. The brain makes no distinction among emotional, physical, and intellectual threats. When it is threatened, cerebral blood flow slows. Upon relaxation, after about 20 minutes, regular blood flow resumes, and the person can think again. During this time, the blood flow shifts from the frontal lobe to the limbic system. Therefore, if the student is too emotional during a lesson, for any reason, the brain becomes overwhelmed with hormones, including adrenaline, and it becomes difficult to focus or make decisions. If too little emotion is involved in learning, the students will not be able to attend to what is going on around them.

Teaching strategies for accessing the emotional memory pathway include:

- Celebrate!
- Use humor (though not sarcasm).
- Debate.
- Use music to change moods.
- Use role-play.
- Create simulations
- Play games.
- Have fun!
- Art.

Although there are many other things that affect memory, these are the four pathways to get there. In the remainder of this book, we will look at ways to organize lessons so that you can efficiently tap into these pathways and help students learn.

In her book, *Worksheets Don't Grow Dendrites* Marcia Tate (2003) states that the literal definition of sarcasm is "a tearing of the flesh." The definition is especially appropriate since remarks directed to students that demean, tease, or deride can, at minimum, hinder or incapacitate higher-level thinking. (p. 37)

PART II
The Lesson Plan

When I was doing my student teaching, it took me hours to make lesson plans. For me, lesson plans were not about preparing good, thorough ways to teach something. Instead, they were tedious exercises in stating the obvious. I thought they were painful. Once I started teaching, my lesson plans became sketchier and sketchier. It didn't mean I wasn't going to do fun, innovative things with my lessons, simply that no one could tell by looking at my plans anything about what I was going to do. Because I did the lesson planning so poorly, the lessons themselves weren't always as complete as they should have been. I often overlooked important steps while inventing on the fly.

A lot of my problem with the lesson planning was my attitude. I had decided that writing everything down was a waste of time; therefore I was going to do as little of it as possible. Once a person gets a bad attitude about something, it takes a concerted effort to change it—and I did not bother trying. However, I believe that part of my attitude came from the very cumbersome lesson plan format that we had to use.

I first saw the five part model for lesson planning at a conference where Richard Allen was presenting (Allen & Kelly, 2004). I was amazed! I thought it made everything so easy. Why, you could just plug an activity into each category and the plan practically writes itself! The remainder of this book is just that: suggested activities that can be used for each step of the lesson plan. First, though, we need to look at the format of the plan to understand the purpose of each of these steps, and how they all fit together to form the big picture.

> The lesson plan format in the remainder of this book is based on that proposed by Richard Allen (2002) in his book *Impact Teaching*. Although he does not claim that the model is specifically based on brain research, it is engaging and keeps the students mentally, physically, socially, or emotionally involved in every step of the lesson.

■ THE FIVE-PART MODEL FOR LESSON PLANS

> The times listed for each of these components of the lesson plan are only suggestions and are extremely flexible. For example, the engager for my lessons often takes half an hour or more. If this is the case, I try to ensure that the engager itself is tied to the lesson at hand. In addition, I often cycle through the model during the course of a lesson, having more than one frame, activity, or debrief during the class session.

1. Engager (2–5 minutes)

Used to engage the students' attention, this is deliberately inserted into the lesson to help prepare the students for learning. It is a brief activity to cause a change of state in the students and help them to mentally leave their "baggage" behind. This step helps the instructor to quickly grab the attention of the learners, and helps students to fully attend to the situation at hand.

2. Frame (< 1minute)

Used to create an appropriate perspective, this section of the lesson plan helps the learner to answer the questions: Why should I attend to this topic? What will it matter to me? The frame should be at the beginning of the lesson so that the students have a reason to pay attention.

3. Activity (5–30 minutes)

Note that the root word to this is *active*. The experience introduces the basic ideas or concepts being taught. Learning should be an active process: mentally, kinesthetically, socially, emotionally, or some combination of these. It should be a creative process in conjunction with some instruction apart from lecture.

4. Debrief (5–15 minutes)

This is the component of the lesson in which the teaching points are highlighted or clarified. The students discover and integrate key aspects of the activity for themselves. The experience and conversation is narrowed down to the key points, making sure that everyone understands the meanings of the activity.

5. Story and Metaphor  (2–5 minutes)

Here the instructor ensures that the material is made "real" to the student by including a story, metaphor, or other device. This gives the students something to "hang their hats on." It also helps them to view the information from a broader perspective.

One can easily imagine that there are many possibilities for each of these steps, depending on the topic at hand. What follows in the remainder of this book are suggestions as to how each of the steps can be taught. This is not meant to be a definitive, exhaustive list of activities; rather, they are examples to get you started. You will want to use your own ideas to suit your own personality as well as that of your class. In addition, these ideas will need to be adapted and expanded upon to fit the topic you are teaching. I have personally used these activities in my classes, and I teach teenagers and adults. There is no upper limit as to the age when most of these are appropriate, and the majority of them will even be appropriate for upper elementary school children. Everyone likes to have fun while learning, and all students learn better when they are enjoying themselves. Please make these suggestions your own and adapt them as you see fit. Above all—enjoy yourself!

2

Engager

Lasting only 2–5 minutes, this portion of the lesson plan is meant to help the students leave behind all the problems they had when they walked into the classroom. This activity can serve one or two purposes: You can use it simply to get the students energized and focused on the class, or it can also be used to access prior knowledge.

All learners come to school, and hence, to your class, burdened with a variety of things on their minds. What they are thinking about depends upon several things, such as the age of your students and the area in which they live. However, they are all thinking about something other than math (or social studies, or grammar, or whatever you teach) when they enter your door. The teacher needs to do something to quickly grab their attention and prepare them for learning. You should incorporate as much movement into lessons as

In *Understanding by Design,* Grant Wiggins and Jay McTighe (1998) advise teachers to "Hook the student through engaging and provocative entry points" (p. 116). Madeline Hunter (2004) calls the engager the "anticipatory set." In *Mastery Teaching,* she states:

. . . take advantage of the beginning of your class to create an anticipatory set that will take your students' minds off of other things and focus their attention on that day's content. An anticipatory set is an activity that brings mental focus (activates the neural programs necessary) to the upcoming learning activity. An anticipatory set may hook into and bring forward students' past knowledge and experiences, which facilitates the acquisition of that day's learning. An anticipatory set may also provide valuable diagnostic information about the knowledge or skills the students already possess, their cognitive, affective, or psycho-motor entry behavior. (p. 40)

possible, especially in this section. Movement increases the heart rate, which, in turn, increases the amount of blood flow to the brain. Movement also increases energy, elevates mood, decreases stress, and decreases fatigue. The following is a collection of brief activities designed to cause a change of state in the students and help them to mentally leave their "baggage" behind. This in no way is meant to be a comprehensive compilation of activities for this step of the lesson plan, but it should help to get you started in using this lesson plan model. Soon you will be generating ideas of your own that suit your needs even better than these do.

Research for each of elements that engage the brain in these energizers can be found at the end of the book.

1. Interview: Man on the Street

THIS ACTIVITY USES

- accessing prior knowledge
- building community
- movement
- question development
- social interaction
- summarization

Objective

Students will conduct interviews with one another to learn something new about each other, hone note-taking skills, and tap into prior knowledge about the subject soon to be taught.

Time Required

Approximately 15 minutes, depending on the number of students participating and prior knowledge of the subject.

Materials

None

Procedure

1. Divide the students into two groups (see Chapter 7, "How to Mix a Group").

2. One of the groups will be reporters; the other, "persons on the street."

3. The reporters are told to find a person on the street and ask three questions. They will want to take notes.

4. Tell the students that two of the questions will be about something personal; the other question will be about something pertaining to the subject to be taught. You may want to assign a specific question and review what is an appropriate and an inappropriate question to ask someone.

5. The students should interview at least three people. Give them four or five minutes for this.

6. Have an agreed upon signal (e.g., flip the lights, play and turn off music) that will indicate that everyone should switch roles. You may want to allow the second students a little less time (three to four minutes.)

Variations

- Give the students a couple of minutes to write down questions to ask before beginning the activity.
- Divide the class into pairs and have them only ask questions of each other. (This will minimize the time necessary for the activity.)

Discuss

- What have the students learned about each other?
- What prior knowledge was gleaned about the subject?
- What effect did note-taking have on the activity?

EXAMPLE

In a class where the students are about to study the Great Depression era, group A can ask what the Depression was; group B can ask when it took place.
The questions may be something like:

1. What is your name?

2. What did you have for breakfast today?

3. What was the Great Depression?

Or

1. What is your name?

2. Do you have any brothers or sisters?

3. Where did the Great Depression take place?

2. Who Am I?

THIS ACTIVITY USES

- accessing prior knowledge
- movement
- novelty
- question development
- social interaction

Objective

Students will try to ascertain the identity of the person, place, thing, or incident (you could even use math formulas) taped to their backs by asking yes or no questions.

Time Required

5–15 minutes, depending on how familiar the students are with what they are guessing.

Materials

A picture or word to tape to each student's back.

Procedure

1. Tape a picture or word to each student's back, making sure that they cannot see it.

2. Instruct the students to find out the identity of what is taped to their backs.

3. They may ask only yes and no questions, and they may only ask each person one question until they have asked everyone in the class. Then they can start asking questions of those whom they have asked before.

4. When several people have guessed their names, stop the game.

Variations

- These can be very general, or you can work on prior knowledge by using subject matter with which they will already be familiar.
- Allow a specified amount of time for the game.

Discuss

- Each person should have an opportunity to tell the class about the person, location, thing, or incident on his or her back.
- Ask the students what the pictures or labels all have in common to lead into the lesson.

EXAMPLE

When working on a unit on the Masters of Impressionistic art, you could put the names of the artists on the students' backs. The students would then ask questions such as: "Was the person female?" "Was the person insane?" "Did the person paint ballerinas?" After the game is over, the students tell the class who they had and what they know about the artist. Ask the rest of the class if they know more.

3. Reporter Relay

THIS ACTIVITY USES

- art
- competition
- making comparisons
- movement
- social interaction

Objective

Half of the students will try to draw a picture based on the description the others give them.

Time Required

About 5 minutes.

Materials

Pictures, paper, and crayons or markers. The pictures can be general works of art, or they can be specific to the lesson you are about to teach. You can have everyone work on the same picture, or have each team draw something different.

Procedure

1. Divide the class into pairs and designate one person in the pair to be the artist; the other will be the reporter.

2. Instruct the artists to sit at desks or tables at one end of the room with the art supplies.

3. On the other end of the room give each reporter a picture, but don't let him or her look at it yet. You may want to have the pictures taped to desks with a blank sheet of paper over them.

4. Inform the class that the artists are going to draw what the reporters tell them to. The artists may not look at the pictures they are copying, and the reporters may not carry the pictures away from the designated area. Make sure the pictures are several feet away from the artists.

5. Set a timer for a short amount of time (maybe three minutes, depending on the amount of detail in the picture).

6. When time is up, display the pictures with the originals.

Variation

- You may want to have an impartial judge decide whose drawing most nearly copies the original.

Discuss

- Why was it more difficult to tell someone what to draw, than to just draw it?
- Why was it more difficult to draw what someone was telling you, than if you could see the picture for yourself?
- If the distance from the picture to the artist made a difference, why?
- How were frustrations handled together?
- If you used pictures that correspond with your lesson, what are their significance?

EXAMPLE

When beginning a unit on the Revolutionary War, have the teams draw "The Declaration of Independence," by John Trumball. When the students are finished drawing the clipart, talk about who the people in the picture are and their significance in the event.

4. Do You Know Your Neighbor?

THIS ACTIVITY USES

- building community
- competition
- humor
- laughter
- movement
- social interaction

Objective

Students will find things that many of them have in common.

Time Required

5–15 minutes.

Materials

Chairs for all students arranged in a large circle.

Procedure

1. Arrange the chairs in a circle. Make sure that there is a chair for each student.

2. The instructor must start the activity by standing inside the circle and making a statement that begins with, "I have a neighbor who . . ." An example of this would be, "I have a neighbor who is wearing white socks."

3. Everybody to whom the statement pertains (i.e., everybody wearing white socks) must stand up and change seats. The person in the middle must make a statement that pertains to him, because he must also scramble to get a seat.

4. The person who couldn't find a seat will be the new person to be in the middle, and must make a statement in turn.

5. When you change seats, you cannot take a seat immediately adjacent to the one in which you are currently sitting.

Variation

- You may allow the students to make general "I have a neighbor . . . " statements, or give them a topic (e.g., rules about triangles).

Discuss

- If being the person in the middle isn't difficult, why does everyone work so hard to avoid being "it"?

- If topics were given, discuss the answers after each statement. (This exercise could also be used for a review.)

EXAMPLE

The instructor starts in the middle saying, "I have a neighbor who wears brown shoes to school." Everyone who has on brown shoes has to change places. Remember, the person in the middle has to say something that pertains to herself, so that she, too, can find a new seat.

5. Corners

THIS ACTIVITY USES

- accessing prior knowledge
- building community
- movement
- sharing opinions
- social interaction

Objective

The students will move to a different corner of the room, according to their position on a topic.

Time Required

Varies by topic. At least 2 minutes.

Materials

None.

Procedure

1. Designate different corners of the room as being different opinions or even different facts.

2. Make a statement and have the students stand in the corner that they feel best represents their answer.

Variation

- You can use this for a variety of purposes. For example, you can mix a group (e.g., different corners represent different birth months), see what they know about a topic, or see how comfortable they are with a topic.

Discuss

- Within the groups: Discuss why you chose your position on the topic.
- The students of different groups can explain their positions to one another.
- A representative from each group can participate in a fishbowl discussion (see next activity).

EXAMPLE

To find what the students think about government foreign policies before you start discussing the policies in class, assign different opinions to different corners, or "strongly agree" to one wall and "strongly disagree" to another wall. This will allow you and the students to get a visual of where members of the class stand on issues. After the lesson, play the game again to see if any of the opinions have changed.

6. Fishbowl Discussion

THIS ACTIVITY USES

- accessing prior knowledge
- provoking curiosity
- social interaction

Objective

The students will both participate in and observe a conversation about a topic or topics.

Time Required

5–10 minutes.

Materials

Have one to three topics prepared to discuss.

Procedure

1. Choose five people to begin in the center of the group and ask them to move their chairs into a circle in the center (see Chapter 7, "How to Mix a Group").

2. Ask the rest of the students to put their chairs in a larger circle around the previously mentioned five.

3. Pose the first question or topic and ask those in the middle of the group to begin the discussion.

4. After a couple of minutes, remove two or three of the students from the middle and replace them with people from the outside ring, using the same method you used to select the first students.

5. Continue removing and replacing students as the conversation continues. When the discussion starts to wane, change the topic.

Variations

- You can move the entire interior group all at once or replace them one at a time.
- Although it is best to begin with a general or current event topic, the topics can gradually be lead to the subject that will soon be studied.

Discuss

- As a group, talk about how the discussions went and if there are points that weren't covered adequately.

EXAMPLE

Start the fishbowl discussion by talking about something the students are all interested in, like a sporting event that is soon going to occur in the school. After a couple of minutes, change some of the participants and ask a question that will segue into the next lesson.

7. Fill 'er Up

THIS ACTIVITY USES

- accessing prior knowledge
- competition
- movement
- social interaction
- time limit

Objective

The students will compete to write as many words related to a particular topic as they can, given time constraints.

Time Required

2–3 minutes.

Materials

Chalkboard or dry-erase board and appropriate writing utensils.

Procedure

1. Divide the class into two teams (see Chapter 7, "How to Mix a Group") and divide the board in half.

2. Tell them that this will be a relay. Only one person from each team (the one with the chalk or marker) is allowed to be standing at a time.

3. When you say "Go," the students will take turns going to the board and writing one word that relates to the topic.

4. Once they have written on the board, the students will go back to their groups and hand the chalk or marker to the next person in line.

5. When the time is up, the group with the most words wins. (No words that are repeated on a team are counted.)

Variations

- You can put the subject of the current unit on the board and have the students write words related to the unit.
- Spelling counts. If a word is spelled incorrectly, it is disqualified.

Discuss

- Discuss the words on the board as you are counting them. If there is any doubt as to why a word would be related to the topic, have the students who wrote the words justify them.

EXAMPLE

Choose a generic topic, such as "fruit." Write the topic near the top of the board and draw a big "T" under it. Each team will write their words on one side of the "T." After the time has expired, count the words for each side.

Now play again, this time choosing the subject you are about to study. For instance, if you have been studying *The Odyssey*, write this on the board and instruct the students to write words that pertain to the plot, reminding them that they will need to justify their words at the end.

8. Word Play

THIS ACTIVITY USES

- accessing prior knowledge
- social interaction
- time limit

Objective

The students will think of as many words as they can that are related to particular categories and beginning with specific letters.

Time Required

Totally depends on what you want to ask. At least 5 minutes, but can be much more.

Materials

You will need one basket (or other container) with possible topics and another with the letters of the alphabet. The topics should be extremely general and have many possibilities associated with it, such as school words, first names of boys, American cities, and so forth. Also, each student needs a pencil and paper.

Procedure

1. Choose a topic and a letter from the baskets.

2. Tell the students that they will have 1 minute to get as many words in each category that they can, but their words can begin only with the designated letters.

3. Set the timer for 1 minute. Much more than that will send the students into frustration.

4. When the time is up, each person counts his or her words. Words only count if no one else has them. Ask the students what their words were by going around the room. The person with the most unique words wins.

Variations

- You may choose up to three letters and up to three topics. If you use more letters and topics, you might want to allow more time.
- As a segue into the next lesson, you can connect the final topic(s), linking what they know about the topic to be taught to what they already know about the subject.

Discuss

- If you used this activity as a link between a past lesson and what you are about to do, discuss the relationships they have with one another.

EXAMPLE

Start with a general topic, such as kitchen words. Draw a letter out of the basket and set the timer. Go around the class and see what words people thought of. Next, make the subject more closely related to the upcoming topic, such as math words. Set the timer again. When the time is up, go around the class again to ascertain the words the class came up with. If necessary, have them justify how their words fit with the topic.

9. Scavenger Hunt

THIS ACTIVITY USES

- competition
- cooperative learning
- movement
- social interaction

Objective

The students will find objects around the room or area.

Time Required

Totally depends on how many things you hide and how difficult you make the hunt.

Materials

Depending on the size of the class, you will want to hide at least three clues and a final object for every third person.

Procedure

1. Decide where you are going to hide the final objects and work backward.
2. Hide at least three clues that will lead the students to the final object.
3. Divide the class into groups of three (see Chapter 7, "How to Mix a Group").
4. Have the students within the groups work together to follow the clues to the final object.

Variations

- Have objects that all relate to one another in some way. The game is not over until the groups come to a consensus about the relationship.
- If possible, consider taking the class outside, or outside the classroom, for this activity.

Discuss

- What do the objects have in common?
- How do they all relate to the topic?

EXAMPLE

For an upcoming lesson in pioneers, hide pictures of pickaxes, wagon wheels, horses, camping equipment, firearms, and so forth. When the students find their clues, they need to share them with the rest of the class by hanging them on the blackboard. The first group that figures out what the next topic will be wins.

10. Dialogue Circles

THIS ACTIVITY USES

- accessing prior knowledge
- building community
- movement
- social interaction

Objective

The students will be able to talk on a given subject without interruption.

Time Required

Totally depends on what you want to ask. At least 2 minutes, but can be much more.

Materials

None.

Procedure

1. Divide the class into two equal groups (see Chapter 7, "How to Mix a Group"). If there is an odd number in the group, the instructor should participate to even the numbers out.

2. Have the class form two concentric circles—half of the class will stand in a circle facing out, the other half of the class in a circle around the first circle. Each of the students should be directly facing a student in the opposing circle.

3. Tell the students that they will be given a topic and that the inside circle must talk on the topic, uninterrupted, until the time is up. Those on the outside will simply listen.

4. Set the timer. At first, it is uncomfortable to talk without feedback, so don't give them much time (10–20 seconds will probably be sufficient).

5. Assign the topic. You can adjust, add, or subtract the time according to how the conversations seem to be going.

6. When time is up, allow the outside people to speak, but on a different topic.

7. Have one of the circles rotate one person to the left, so each person is now speaking with someone new. Restart the conversation, but change the topic. (Hint: You must change topics, or the first listener will be planning what they want to say rather than listening.)

8. If you want to continue the activity, have the other circle rotate in the opposite direction and assign a new topic.

Variation

- Start the topics with something personal and segue into the topic you are about to teach.

Discuss

- As a whole group, discuss the prior knowledge accessed in the conversations.

EXAMPLE

When continuing a unit on the writing process, start out with something general. For instance, have the first speakers talk about their routine when they get up in the morning. Next, have the second speakers tell about what they do when they get home. When the students seem to warm up (that is, they are talking more freely), have one of them talk about the steps in the writing process. The next set will talk about the specific step you will be working on during the lesson. This will help the students to be prepared for the work to come.

11. What's Missing?

THIS ACTIVITY USES

- metacognition
- visuals

Objective

The students will try to remember a collection of items on display and identify changes.

Time Required

5 minutes.

Materials

A collection of materials; it is best to put 10–12 items on a tray. You may want to have generic, unrelated items the first time you play, and items that relate to your subject matter the next time.

Procedure

1. Slowly walk by each person with the tray of items, allowing everyone a couple of seconds to look at them.

2. Move out of sight of the class and remove one to three of the items.

3. Again, move among the students with the tray, allowing them to see what is on it.

4. Have the students write what they think is missing.

5. As a class, review the missing items.

Variations

- Play "Corners" to have the students identify what they thought was missing.
- Display the times on an overhead projector.

Discuss

- What do the items have in common?
- For those who guessed correctly, how did they remember the missing items?
- What would have made this game easier? (Try to get them to say that taking notes, grouping the items, or devising a mnemonic of some kind would have helped.)

EXAMPLE

Before a geometry lesson, put several items of various geometric shapes on a tray. For example: a coin, a sticky note, a pen, a ball, and so forth. Have the students look at the items, and then covertly remove a couple of them. Allow the students to look at the tray again. Remind them not to verbalize their responses; they need to write them down. Review the missing items. As a lead into the lesson, help the students group the items by geometric shapes.

12. Mystery Box

THIS ACTIVITY USES

- cooperative learning
- making inferences
- provoking curiosity
- question development

Objective

The students will ask a series of yes–no questions to discover what is in a box. This can be used as a review of a previous lesson or a preview of an upcoming one.

Time Required

Several minutes, but can be spread out over a period of time.

Materials

You will need a large box with something in it pertaining to a lesson.

Procedure

1. Present to the class a large box.

2. Tell them that the box has something in it and that it will be their job to discover what it is. However, they can only ask yes and no questions.

3. Periodically throughout the day, go around and have the students ask questions about the box. You may want to allow them to pick it up.

4. When they make their final guesses, they should also guess how the item is connected with the subject at hand.

Variations

- Have the students justify their answers when they make guesses.
- Instruct the students to give an explanation for the use of each item they guess.
- Limit the students' guesses or make them unlimited.
- Assign pairs or groups and have them ask the questions and make their guesses together.

Discuss

- What was the process by which the students formed their guesses?
- For what was the item actually used?

EXAMPLE

When beginning a lesson on life cycles, put an egg in the box and have the students guess what it is. You may want to boil it if you are going to do the guessing over a couple of days.

13. Crossed Wires: Telephone With a Twist

THIS ACTIVITY USES

- accessing prior knowledge
- laughter
- movement
- novelty
- social interaction

Objective

The teacher will give a number of sentences to different people in the class and have them pass the sentences around the room.

Time Required

2–3 minutes.

Materials

Two to five prewritten sentences.

Procedure

1. Select from two to five students and orally give them each different sentences; do this in such a way that the rest of the class can't hear.

2. Direct these students to each tell one other student the sentence.

3. Have the students systematically pass the sentences around the room. (You may want the class to stand in a circle or in groups.)

4. Ask the last student to receive each of the sentences to repeat what he or she heard.

Variations

- Start out by playing Telephone, but add more messages as the game progresses.
- Add the additional messages sporadically throughout the "telephone line."
- Send the additional messages the other way down the telephone line.

Discuss

- Why do the messages get confused?
- What would have made this activity easier?
- How does this activity relate to the real world?

EXAMPLE

To begin an economics lesson, the first couple of messages should be general and rather short, like: The sky is blue. The next sentence will be more complicated and better related to the upcoming subject. "Price is set by a formula of supply and demand." "High gas prices can cause cost-push inflation." As you finish the exercise, discuss the final sentences and use them as a lead to the lesson.

14. Collaborative Stories

THIS ACTIVITY USES

- cooperative learning
- imagination
- movement
- time limit
- writing

Objective

The students will write with logical event sequences.

Time Required

5–15 minutes.

Materials

Different pictures for each group; pencils and paper.

Procedure

1. Divide students into groups of three to five.

2. Give each group a picture. This works best if the picture has a lot of action in it.

3. Give the students 2–3 minutes to begin a story with their picture.

4. Leaving the picture and story on the table, direct the students to change tables so they will be working with a different story. Each time they change stories, give them a little more time, so they can read what is already there.

5. Tell the students when it is the last turn to write, so they can create an ending to the story on which they are currently working.

6. Have the students return to their original story. Have each group read their stories aloud.

Variations

- Instead of giving them a picture, you could give each group an opening sentence.
- You can specify the type of story they write.
- Have a student in each group illustrate the story.
- Give each group the same picture, so they can see the different types of ideas they can generate from one picture.
- The picture can be of a period or subject you are about to discuss.

Discuss

- Why is it difficult to follow someone else's writing?
- Is it easier to write in groups or on your own? Why?

EXAMPLE

Before continuing the lesson on World War II, gather several pictures depicting different scenes: dog fighting airplanes, women working in factories, the D-Day assault, and so forth. Have the students write stories about these scenes. Use the stories as you introduce each of the scenarios in the lesson.

15. To Tell the Truth

THIS ACTIVITY USES

- building community
- emotion
- inference
- novelty
- question development

Objective

This is just like the old television game show. One student has an unusual experience or talent; three students participate on a panel and answer yes and no questions as the rest of the class tries to identify which student is not lying.

Time Required

5–15 minutes.

Materials

None.

Procedure

1. Instruct the students to write on a piece of paper something that they don't think anyone else in the class knows about them. This could be something they can do, an experience they have had, or something as simple as what they had for dinner the evening before. They should also put their names on the paper.

2. The instructor will choose one of the "talented" students and two others to be on the panel. The talented one will tell the others about his or her experience.

3. The instructor will tell the class what the talent or experience is.

4. The other students in the class will take turns questioning the panel, one at a time. Each person in the audience can ask questions for a set amount of time (less than a minute) of only one person at a time.

5. Each of the students on the panel will try to answer as though the experience were his or hers.

6. When everyone has had a chance to ask a question, have the students guess by applause when you hold your hand over the panelists' heads.

Variations

- Instead of having the whole class ask questions individually, you could have the students ask their questions as groups.

- Instead of having a panel, have only one student on the "hot seat" and the rest of the class guess what their secret is.
- Have the students on the panel role-play people you are studying in class. Have the class figure out who the panelists are role-playing.

Discuss

- Why were the students fooled? Why were they not fooled?

EXAMPLE

Of the three students on the panel, Aaron, Tina, and Trent, only Aaron has been to Mount Rushmore. The job of the class is to figure out this difference. They take turns asking yes or no questions of each of the panelists until someone figures it out.

16. Quick Draw

THIS ACTIVITY USES

- accessing prior knowledge
- art
- competition
- cooperative learning
- laughter
- time limit

Objective

The students will race to draw pictures of concepts and have their teams guess the words. This is very similar to the game "Pictionary."

Time Required

About 30 seconds per word; the amount of time this activity takes depends on how many words you want to use.

Materials

Large chalkboard or dry-erase board; words to draw written on slips of paper.

Procedure

1. Divide the students into two teams.

2. Instruct the students that they will take turns drawing a picture of the words they are given.

3. Have one student from each team come to the front of the room and, without looking, pick a slip of paper with the drawing idea.

4. Time the students. Each competing pair of students has a given amount of time to draw the pictures and have their teammates identify them.

5. Signal for the students to start drawing.

6. The audience of each team must guess what was drawn.

7. The first team to guess correctly wins; if no one guesses within the time limit, both competitors sits down and a new person from each team comes to the front.

Variations

- Give the two teams different words to draw.
- Have the students draw concepts related to what you are about to study.
- Allow the artists to describe their artwork, or force them to remain mute.

Discuss

- Discuss any words the students had trouble drawing. Remember that if they do not really understand the vocabulary, they can't draw it.
- If you are using this to access prior knowledge of an upcoming unit or topic, ask the students what the words had in common.

EXAMPLE

As a way to review vocabulary words, put all of the target words in a basket and give them to the representatives of the teams. They can only draw the words if they really understand them. This will also give you an opportunity to see with which words the students are having problems.

17. Categories

THIS ACTIVITY USES

- accessing prior knowledge
- competition
- making connections
- social interaction
- time limit

Objective

The students will try to guess what a series of words have in common.

Time Required

1 minute per series.

Materials

An overhead with a list of related words (four to eight) on a transparency.

Procedure

1. Divide the students into pairs (see Chapter 7, "How to Mix a Group").

2. Have the class sit so that half of them are facing the overhead and half have their backs to it.

3. Display the overhead, telling the students that they can't talk to their partner until the time is set. They will have one minute.

4. Start the timer.

5. The students can read the words through once. If their partners cannot guess what the words have in common (the series title), they can add clues. However, they cannot use part of, or a form of, the title in the clues.

6. The first team to correctly guess the category wins.

Variation

- You may use general words for each series or words from an upcoming unit or chapter to access prior knowledge.

Discuss

- The series and their commonalities.
- If you used words to lead into a lesson, discuss how they relate to what you are about to study.

EXAMPLE

Before a science lesson, begin the period by dividing the class and putting a list on the overhead, such as *buildings, sidewalks, parks, people, skyscrapers, traffic, lights,* and *streets.* The first person gives the clues; the second person guesses. Do a few of these, changing readers and guessers, so that everyone has had the opportunity to guess a couple of times. Next, put words up that relate to the lesson: *petal, stigma, anther, filament, style, ovary, ovule,* and *nectar* (parts of a flower). Have the students guess this and other words that pertain to the upcoming lesson.

18. Lifeboat

THIS ACTIVITY USES

- accessing prior knowledge
- building community
- cooperative learning
- inference

Objective

The students will listen to a scenario and evaluate the tools and items they think will be necessary for survival.

Time Required

5–15 minutes.

Materials

A short scenario, perhaps two to four paragraphs long. This scenario should outline an event or catastrophe that will happen.

Procedure

1. Divide the class into teams with three to five people (see Chapter 7, "How to Mix a Group").

2. Tell students that you are going to read a scenario and that they should decide within the groups the items they will want to take.

3. Limit the items they will take (e.g., each group can take a certain number of items, a certain weight, or a certain bulk, such as only one paper bag).

4. Give each group 3–5 minutes to discuss what they will bring and why.

5. Go around the class and have the groups report on their decisions and give their reasons for them.

6. Read the rest of the scenario to ascertain which of the groups would have survived.

Variation

- The scenarios can be fantasy, on a topic you are about to study, or something from their lives.

Discuss

- Discuss the reasons the groups give for their decisions and the kinds of end scenarios that would require the items the students selected.

- Once you finish reading the scenarios, discuss who would be most likely to survive and why.
- Discuss how they adapt the items they chose to fit the needs of the situation.
- Discuss how this relates to real life.

EXAMPLE

In the middle of a unit on immigration, begin the day's lesson on what a family of immigrants in the early twentieth century, consisting of a mother, father, and four small children, could take with them. They had to be able to carry everything, and they would have to sail at least 2 months on a boat before arriving. The immigrants were extremely poor and would not be able to buy anything upon arrival until they had jobs and earned the money they would need. Divide the class into groups and have them decide what to bring. They need to be prepared to justify their choices.

After everyone has decided, finish the story: The youngest child fell and broke a leg the second day onboard. Who brought things that could be used to set the leg?

19. Hot Potato

THIS ACTIVITY USES

- accessing prior knowledge
- laughter
- movement
- novelty
- social interaction
- time limit

Objective

The students will pass a ball around a circle while a timer is running.

Time Required

2–3 minutes.

Materials

Timer and a small object to pass.

Procedure

1. Have students stand in a circle.
2. Set a timer for 10–20 seconds.
3. Have students pass the object around the circle, trying not to be the one holding it when the timer goes off.
4. When the timer buzzes, the student holding the object will have to do something.

Variations

- You may have the students tell their name or something about themselves.
- You may also want the students to say something they know about the upcoming session.

Discuss

- Discuss how it made them feel each time they held the object. Why?

EXAMPLE

In an English as a Second Language class, pass the object (we use a beanbag cow). The person left holding the cow when the timer goes off has to answer a question pertaining what he or she has been studying. For instance, the instructor names a preposition and the student has to demonstrate it: As an example, the instructor says "Inside," and the student steps inside the circle; "beside" and the student says, "I am beside Maria"; "outside" and the student steps outside the circle.

20. Two Truths and a Lie

THIS ACTIVITY USES

- building community
- emotion
- inference
- novelty
- social interaction

Objective

The students will try to determine which of three statements is the truth.

Time Required

2–3 minutes.

Materials

None.

Procedure

1. Have students write two personal statements on a piece of paper that are false and one that is true.

2. Ask them to cut or tear the sentences apart so that they can mix them up in any order.

3. Ask for volunteers to read their sentences to the class.

4. Have the class vote on which sentence is true for each student.

DO NOT use subject matter with this exercise. If you have the students lie about the subject matter (for instance, saying something like "Benjamin Franklin was the third president of the United States") it is likely that they will remember the lie instead of the actual facts.

Variations

- Don't discuss which sentences are true until several students have read their statements.
- Have the students break up into groups and read the sentences among the groups.

Discuss

- Was it difficult to tell whether someone was lying?
- Discuss the importance of body language and being able to read it.

EXAMPLE

Jeff wrote on his paper:

I have a dog.
I have broken nearly every bone in my body.
I hate Chinese food.

The other students would have to guess which of these is true. This is a good exercise for helping the students get to know one another.

3

The Frame

The purpose of the frame is to give the students a reason for learning the upcoming subject matter. There has to be a motive for them to learn it, or else the brain will not be able to keep the information in long-term memory.

When framing the information for the students, you should answer the following questions: Why are they going to spend time on this topic? How does this topic relate to material previously learned, or that which is yet to come? How might the information be useful to them in their personal lives now? How may this material be useful in the future? In essence, how is knowing this information going to improve their lives or make their lives easier? Answering these questions provides a necessary hook for the students to use in processing the information in their brains, thereby allowing the students a pathway for handling what they are about to learn.

The frame is positioned at the beginning of the lesson and should take less than a minute. The instructor simply gives the students a reason to attend to the information, and then moves on to the activity. Make sure the students can answer the question: WIIFM? (What's In It For Me?)

> The brain either pays attention to or disengages from the stimulus based on how intensely the task grabs attention. Many students have a greater impetus for learning when the activity is linked to an issue of personal relevance.
>
> —Gayle H. Gregory and Terence Parry (2006) *Designing Brain-Compatible Learning*, p. 237

> Madeline Hunter (2004), in her book *Mastery Teaching: Increasing Instructional Effectiveness in Elementary and Secondary Schools* states, "Students usually will expend more effort and consequently increase their learning if they know what it is they will learn today and why it is important to them." (p. 38)

SOCIAL STUDIES EXAMPLE

Before beginning the unit on the causes of the Great Depression, discuss with the class the many reasons for why it is important to understand the mistakes and events that led up to, and exacerbated, the era. What is true of the macro economy (the big picture) is often true of the micro economy (the individual business or person). By learning how many of the problems could have been avoided, we can avoid repeating the same mistakes in our own lives.

MATH EXAMPLE

If you were going to paint the inside of your house, how would you know how much paint to buy? By learning how to figure such things as area and perimeter in geometry, you can simplify your life and potentially save yourself a lot of headache—perhaps a lot of money.

SCIENCE EXAMPLE

At the onset of a lesson on geology, open with a discussion about oil and gas prices. Refer to economics and supply and demand. Is there really a finite supply of oil in the world, or is this just a way for the oil companies to make more money? Is there another way to make oil?

LITERATURE EXAMPLE

By being able to find cause and effect in literature, we will be able to identify it in our own lives and thus be able to avoid a lot of problems.

WRITING EXAMPLE

When introducing a writing web, explain to the students that they will no longer have to worry about paragraphing. Using a writing web will take care of that for them. Writing webs make a difficult task manageable and simplifies two of the most difficult tasks of the writing process: coming up with ideas and organizing them.

HEALTH EXAMPLE

By understanding our bodies and how they work, you can avoid being taken advantage of by people making up scientific "facts" that are not really true. If we have knowledge of how things actually function, we can learn to avoid major problems and maximize our health.

4

Activity

Note that the base word used here is *active*. Students should be involved in the process in some way: emotionally, mentally, physically, or socially. This is the step in which the concept is demonstrated in action.

As you begin to know your students better, you will learn the types of activities they enjoy; but do not be afraid to expand their horizons a bit, and occasionally work outside their comfort zones. You will not want to do that on a daily basis, but once in a while is good for them—and for you. The activity portion of the lesson can last 5–30 minutes.

The following list is not meant to be comprehensive, but it should give you some ideas on how to go about making this part of your lesson more active.

21. Writing

Writing can be used in a variety of ways to aid in the learning process. Here is a partial list of methods that you may want to consider using in your classroom:

- learning logs
- summaries
- journaling
- learning journals

Opportunities for writing exist in all classes and at every grade level. Student journals are a rich source of information for the teacher, in addition to serving as vehicles for students' reflection while refining their thinking. Although free writing is valuable, there are times when the teacher may wish to add structure by asking the students to respond to questions or to complete sentences.

—Patricia Wolfe (2001), *Brain Matters: Translating Research Into Classroom Practice,* p. 78

Learning Logs

A learning log is a place in which students can keep track of their learning: That is, they can use learning logs to record things they would like to be able to remember from the lesson. You may want to use a learning log only for the subjects in which the students are having problems, or for those subjects that have a lot of rules (e.g., algebraic formulas or English grammar). However, learning logs could also be used for each subject so that the students can keep a record of their progress in all the subjects they are studying. This will really help them retain what they learn, they can use their notes as refreshers, and they will get writing practice.

Summaries

Summaries are a little different from learning logs in that they can be used more frequently, and the students may or may not want to keep the summaries for review. Here, the student will simply and briefly summarize what he or she is learning. One can use summaries in each step of the learning process: at the conclusion of each paragraph, at the conclusion of each section, at the conclusion of each chapter, or at the end of each class. Whereas learning logs are typically used at the end of a lesson, summaries are used with reading.

In *Classroom Instruction that Works,* Robert Marzano, Debra Pickering, and Jane Pollock (2001) extract some generalizations from the research on summarizing:

To effectively summarize, students must delete some information, substitute some information, and keep some information; to do this, students must analyze the information at a fairly deep level, and; being aware of the explicit structure of information is an aid to summarizing information. (pp. 30–32)

Journaling

Journaling can be used in a variety of ways: the students can journal about a particular subject, or an open topic can be used, where the students write about anything they choose. The teacher can respond to the journals in a discussion-like manner, or the journals can be nonresponse, where the teacher simply checks to see that the student has written something but doesn't actually read it. One can really make journaling fit to the character of the class and the instructor. The truly important thing is to get the students writing.

In his book *How the Brain Learns (3rd ed.),* David Sousa (2006) suggests that the students respond to three questions:

1. "What did we learn today about…"

2. "How does this connect or relate to what we already know about…"

3. "How can this help us, or how can we use this information/skill in the future?" (p. 163)

Learning Journals

The main difference between journals and learning journals is the subject. In a learning journal, the students have the opportunity to reflect on, respond to, and give active feedback on what they are learning in class. The students can write about that with which they disagree, about that on which they are unclear, or about what they have concluded or observed about a lesson.

22. Mnemonic Devices

Mnemonic devices are those little things that help you remember sequences, rules, and formulas, such as: "i before e except after c" and PEMDAS (*p*lease *e*xcuse *m*y *d*ear *A*unt *S*ally standing for the order of operations in math: Parentheses, Exponents, Multiplication and Division, Addition and Subtraction). Basically, mnemonic devices are effective ways to use chunking, acronyms, acrostics, or rhymes to aid in memory. The brain is a pattern-seeking device, and mnemonics provide patterns and connections to aid the memory. If you think about it for a minute, you will probably be able to come up with several that you used in elementary school to remember something, and those same mnemonic devices are still the way you remember those things.

There are a couple of ways in which one may use mnemonic devices:

- they can be given to the students
- the students can write their own

Give the Mnemonic Devices

The reason you know what mnemonic devices are is that when you were in school your teachers helped you remember things with them. Many mnemonic devices are passed down from generation to generation, simply because they work. Giving students mnemonic devices to help them remember those difficult-to-remember facts can indeed be of great assistance to them.

> According to Karen Markowitz and Eric Jensen (1999) in *The Great Memory Book,* when people use mnemonics they can double or triple the amount of information they can store in their brains.

Student-Created Mnemonics

Another way to use mnemonic devices in the classroom is to have the students invent their own. Break the students into groups of two or three and have them come up with memorable phrases or rhymes that they can use for the subject matter they are currently learning. Have them make their own acrostics or acronyms for the order of something. There are so many things for which it would be appropriate to use mnemonic devices that the only limitations for this strategy are the imaginations of the students and the teacher.

23. Peer Discussion and Peer Teaching

Students learn much more of what they teach to someone else, as opposed to the small amount they usually learn from their reading. Having the students teach the subject matter to one another just makes good sense. They know the language to use to make a peer understand, and if the students just learned something themselves, they understand the barriers they had to their own learning.

Another good way to use peer teaching is as a feedback tool. Ideally, students should get feedback often—about every 30 minutes (see Chapter 5, "Debrief"). Having them teach one another ensures that everybody is on the same page in understanding the ongoing material.

When you have your students involved in peer teaching, everyone wins—the "learners" get another opportunity to be exposed to the material, and the "teachers" get an opportunity to cement their own learning.

There are many ways to institute peer teaching in your classroom. What follow are a few suggestions.

Ask the Expert

"Ask the Expert" can be done in several different ways. You can have the students pick which aspect of the subject they would each like to investigate further (such as a particular event in history), or you can have the students each read a different section of the material and teach one another their assigned materials. Keep in mind that the students will know the material they teach better than any of the rest, so don't use this on something that is vital for all students to know. For instance, you can use it to teach specific wars that were waged during the Civil War, but not for the assassination of President Lincoln.

> Peer teaching accomplishes several objectives. First, it allows the students an opportunity to rehearse what they have learned, thus strengthening their neural pathways. Also, students are likely to give more attention to the lesson knowing they'll be required to share the information.... Finally, peer teaching provides valuable diagnostic information for the teacher, who finds out how well students comprehend the material and what misconceptions they may have formed. It is much better to discover the misconceptions while you are teaching than to wait until a test to uncover them.
>
> —Patricia Wolfe (2001), *Brain Matters: Translating Research Into Classroom Practice*, pp. 185–186

> In *Brain Compatible Strategies*, Eric Jensen (1997) tells us that "research suggests human subjects learn declarative knowledge ... from unsuccessful performances. In other words, doing it right the first time produces no new learning." Learning and fine-tuning come from doing something over and over. (p. 10)

Shared Reading

The students will read to one another in pairs. This usually works well if they take turns reading paragraphs. However, if the material is particularly difficult to follow, you may want the students to read every other sentence. Shortening the length of material each person is reading helps the students attend to the subject matter, thereby aiding in comprehension. Encourage them to talk about the content as they are reading.

Turn to Your Neighbor and Teach

Finally, you may choose to use "Turn to Your Neighbor and Teach." After teaching something, have the students turn to their close neighbor (you should establish who this will be before beginning the lesson) and tell them what they have just learned. This will ensure that they are all clear on major points and help to keep them attending to the matter at hand. If there are any points on which there is ambiguity, those points will come out at this time.

24. Graphic Organizers

Graphic organizers are visual frames used to represent and organize learning information. They engage students' visual intelligence, stretch students' thinking skills, and promote active learning. Graphic organizers may be used to plan lessons, units, and present information to students. Graphic organizers expand many facets of students' higher level thinking skills including analyzing, synthesizing, evaluating, relating and developing concepts, categorizing, sequencing, and comparing and contrasting.

Graphic organizers also facilitate long-term retention of information. It helps the brain make sense of information and find patterns in the visual cues.

—Kagan Cooperative Learning (2001), *Kagan SmartCards,* taken from the "Graphic Organizers" card

There is an almost unlimited number of ways in which you can use graphic organizers in the classroom. The main purpose behind graphic organizers is to help the students make connections in the relationships among a set of concepts. You may choose to use the graphic organizer as a preview before a lesson, during the lesson to emphasize the progression of the concept, or after the lesson as a debriefing exercise. Here we will discuss a few of the different types of graphic organizers you may use during a lesson.

Concept Tree

With a concept tree, the teacher can draw an illustration of the relationships among the concepts he or she is introducing. A concept tree looks like a family tree, but with ideas rather than names. This works extremely well with subject matter that builds on itself, such as science or social studies.

Grid

To use a grid, simply list a series of events or concepts along the top squares and another type of event or concept along the side. Fill in the grid as the concepts intersect. For instance, write years along the top of the grid and events such as wars, inventions, economy, and society down the side squares. Then fill in the squares according what was happening in each of the categories during each of the years.

Mind Mapping

Although this technique can be used in many subjects, it is extremely helpful when writing. This is the type of graphic organizer that uses bubbles or circles. In the center of the page, write the topic or main idea inside a bubble, similar to a cartoon bubble. As students think of subtopics that go with the main idea, they will write them in surrounding bubbles and connect them to the main idea with lines.

> Presenting students with explicit guidance in identifying similarities and differences enhances students' understanding of and ability to use knowledge.... Asking students to independently identify similarities and differences enhances students' understanding of and ability to use knowledge.
>
> —Robert Marzano, Debra Pickering, and Jane Pollock (2001) *Classroom Instruction That Works*, p. 15

There are many other types of graphic organizers: Venn diagrams, to compare and contrast ideas or events; cycle webs, to demonstrate understanding of cycles and processes; and a cause and effect diagram, to promote explicit relations between what happened and why, are only a few. For some of your students, these webs (or organizers) are not necessary. For others, though, they may make the difference between understanding and being totally lost.

25. Storytelling

It would be difficult to overestimate the value of storytelling in the classroom. Think of the stories you heard as a child. Even if you haven't heard them for years, you can still remember the themes and characters. What is "Cinderella" about? "Little Red Riding Hood?" How about "Hansel and Gretel?" If you knew these when you were a child, chances are you still do. Our brains were built for stories. Therefore, if you can couch the lesson in a story you will not only help the students to understand the concept, you will also help them to remember it.

> Our lives are full of stories. Some of them are positive, some are negative, and all of them can teach us something about the world in which we live. The greater purpose of most learning environments is to increase the quality of the lives of the learners. Stories help students gain insight into how to apply the knowledge and make connections for themselves. Bringing storytelling into the classroom is not only an effective way to teach, it is common sense.
>
> —Richard Allen (2002), *Impact Teaching*, p. 26

I found this out very early in my teaching career. The first 2 years I had my teaching license I made a living by substitute teaching. I really liked the constant variety of it. One day I would be an elementary physical education teacher, the next day I would teach high-school English. I discovered that teaching was pretty much the same, regardless of the age of the student. I also realized that the best discipline plan was a good lesson. The first time I taught elementary physical education I was supposed to do calisthenics with the children. The kids absolutely hated it, and so did I. A couple of weeks later I was back in the same class. This time, instead of calisthenics, I had the children act out a story as I told it to them. I made the story up as I went along and we had a blast. We actually did the exact same calisthenics as before, but this time we did it with imagery. I told them a story about taking a walk (walking in place for a warm up), getting chased by a dog (running in place), picking apples (stretching), picking dandelions (touching toes), and trying to wipe the mud off our knees with our elbows (sit-ups).

That day went so well that I tried the same technique in other classes: middle school science and social studies, high school English, first grade . . . everything I taught in this manner worked. I became a very popular sub with both the children and the teachers, and it was just because I embedded all of the lessons in stories. It works. In fact, it works so well that I just explained the importance of this method by telling you a story. Now I know you understand!

26. Guest Speakers

Occasionally using guest speakers can be a very strong aid to long-term memory. Inviting a guest speaker can be powerful in the classroom because it conveys to the students the importance the instructor places on the topic, gives a different point of view, and allows the students to hear the message from a different voice.

If using a guest speaker is a very rare occurrence, the students will likely see it as a treat and realize that the topic the class is studying is of extreme importance, especially if you emphasize the difficulty the speaker had in making the time to come. You will want to rehearse, prior to the event, how the students will behave for the guest, especially when it's possible they won't understand what the speaker is talking about. It is not uncommon for this to be the case with guests who are not used to teaching, not used to being in a large group, or not used to the age or vocabulary level of the students you teach.

When you decide to invite a guest speaker into your class, it will usually be someone who works in the field or is somehow a specialist. This gives the students a new perspective on the topic.

Also, hearing about the topic from a different voice and seeing a different person allows the students to engage their episodic memories when trying to recall specifics.

Several months ago, I was trying to teach my adult English as a Second Language students about the stock market. They did not understand it at all, so I asked my stockbroker to come in and speak with them. They really did not understand him. He spoke too fast, used the wrong vocabulary, and lectured the whole time. At first glance, it would appear that asking him to come to my class was not a good idea. However, I taught it again the next night. I used the same illustrations and examples the stockbroker had used; just put it in a format that they would understand. They totally got it. With the rehearsals, guest speaker, illustrations, and activities, everybody in the class finally understood. In fact, a couple of them were able to take advantage of the 401(k) and other retirement programs at their places of employment because they realized how these programs worked. If we had not had the guest speaker, I do not believe they would ever have understood.

> Distinct locations and circumstances provide the brain many more identifying clues for efficient retrieval later. The more you utilize this characteristic of spatial-episodic memory, the greater recall your learners will have. Context provides dozens of sensory cues that can better trigger memory.
>
> —Eric Jensen (2004), *Brain Compatible Strategies*, p. 16

27. Movement

Movement is such an integral part of brain-based learning that it is difficult to separate the two. The human brain and body were only made to sit for a limited time, attending to one thing. Your students *will* take a mental vacation; how often, where they go, and when they come back depends upon a variety of factors.

If you are teaching adults, plan to change tactics every 17–22 minutes; the younger the students, the more frequent the guided movement breaks should be.

> ...teachers and administrators need to encourage more movement in all classrooms at all grade levels. At some point in every lesson, students should be up and moving about, preferably talking about their learning. Not only does the movement increase cognitive function, but it also helps students use up some kinesthetic energy so they can settle down and concentrate better later. (p. 233)
>
> ...because trading a few minutes of teacher talk for a movement activity can actually increase the amount of learning retained, it could be a very worthwhile investment of time. (p. 240)
>
> —David Sousa (2006), *How the Brain Learns (3rd ed.)*

This doesn't necessarily mean that you have to change subjects, just that you should give the students' brains a chance to process what they have already learned. Let the students change the focus of their brains so that they don't get "stuck" in a hemisphere, and allow the students to move so that their blood circulates better and can provide more oxygen and fuel for the brain. Movement is also tied strongly to learning. I can still remember all the songs with motions we sang when I was a child in Sunday School, but I can't remember any of the songs without movement. Muscle memory, also known as procedural memory, is one of the four main pathways to the brain. If your students learn a concept while performing a repeated motion, they will be more likely to remember the concept. There are only a couple of drawbacks to this: They will have to repeat the movements, not just the facts, to store the memory in the first place, and the students may have to repeat the motion to recall the memory.

There are many ways to incorporate movement into lessons (see Chapter 8, "Breaks and Energizers"). A couple of strategies that work with movement are incorporating dance (even follow-the-leader) and games into the classroom. Role-playing and pantomime also work with movement; there will be more on these strategies in the next section.

28. Role-Play

Role-play and pantomime work great when you are studying such things as history and drama. However, they also work great when studying science, English, and math.

The reasons for using movement in a classroom also hold true for role-play. In the field of Teaching English as a Second Language there is a very popular technique called TPRS (Total Physical Response Storytelling). This technique is popular because it works so well. In TPRS, the teacher reads

> Watch difficult concepts become easy to understand when students are actively engaged in becoming the concept being taught. For example, elementary students understand the rotation and revolution of the planets as nine children move in circular orbits around one child who has been designated as the sun. High school students comprehend properties of matter as they role play the action of molecules in solids, liquids, and gases.
>
> —Marcia Tate (2003), *Worksheets Don't Grow Dendrites*, p. 85

an extremely short story and acts out the words in simple movements. The students then learn the movements that go with the words, and then act out the story as they read it in unison. They practice the movements and words together several times in a variety of ways (together, in pairs, with eyes closed), and by the end of class they have learned up to 10 words.

This same method also works with other subject matter. When studying history, have the students act out the events that happened. If it is in science, have some of the students work together to demonstrate a concept. In English, each student could hold up a sign to represent a different part of the sentence, paragraph, or story. This will help the students build their spatial intelligence as well as help them to understand the concepts at hand. This also

> Students acquire insights to individuals' lives and perspectives as they role play or impersonate that figure.
>
> —Dr. Spencer and Miguel Kagan (1998), *Multiple Intelligences*, p. 7.24

gives the teacher and the students a chance to incorporate humor into the lesson. Using role-play and pantomime in the classroom is fun; the more the students are enjoying the learning process, the more they are likely to retain.

29. Celebrations

Celebration does not have to mean having a huge party on Valentine's Day or inviting all your students' relatives to school. Instead, incorporate celebration rituals into the everyday life of the class. For example, when the students master a concept, have them turn to one another and say, "Great job!"

Be careful with praise. Although well-deserved praise should be given fluidly, giving praise where it has not been earned will have the opposite effect of what you were hoping. Praise the students after they have done something well, but most important, set them up to praise themselves. Teach the students to be proud of their best efforts and create an atmosphere such that the students praise each other's work.

> In *Classroom Instruction Works*, Marzano, Pickering, and Pollock (2001) make three generalizations, taken from the research, about praise:
>
> 1. Rewards do not necessarily have a negative effect on intrinsic motivation.
>
> 2. Reward is most effective when it is contingent on the attainment of some standard of performance.
>
> 3. Abstract symbolic recognition is more effective than tangible rewards. (pp. 55–59)

30. Debate

Controversy learning, the process of learning by effectively arguing a viewpoint and challenging the opposite view, teaches the students to disagree with one another without losing tempers or getting into arguments. It allows them to express their views, thoughts, and ideas in both oral and written form; emphasizes the need to come prepared with facts; and helps the students to be organized and systematic in their thinking. Improvement in organizational skills and sequential thinking can translate into improvement in other areas, such as better writing organization and paragraphing capabilities.

Like most other techniques, the instructor can use this in a casual or intense manner. Individuals or teams of students can be assigned issues to investigate and debate, or they can choose their own. If you are teaching about American jurisprudence, you could even debate in the guise of a full-fledged court case, where students are appointed to be prosecutors, defense attorneys, witnesses, judge, and jury.

The student debater learns to use a library, and to find the exact information he needs in the shortest possible time. He learns to be thorough and accurate. He learns to analyze; to distinguish between the vital and the unimportant. He learns the need of proving his statements; of supporting every statement with valid evidence and sound reasoning—and he learns to demand the same sort of proof for the statements of others. He learns to present ideas in a clear and effective manner, and in a way which wins others to his way of thinking. He learns to think under pressure, to "use his head" in a time of need, to make decisions quickly and accurately. In a word, the essential point in any debating situation is that of convincing the listener that your side of the proposition is desirable.

—*Debate*, by Harrison Boyd Summers. Retrieved September 23, 2006, from http://ftp.ev1.net/%7Earcwynd/debate/debate.htm

31. Music

The mental mechanisms that process music are deeply entwined with the brain's other basic functions, including emotion, memory, and even language.

—Patricia Wolfe (2001), *Brain Matters: Translating Research Into Classroom Practice*, p. 161

The brain loves order and patterns. Music is patterning, and it can have great effects on what the students hear, what they can remember, and how they perform.

Music can be used before the class begins to create an "atmosphere." Play upbeat music as students are entering the room as a tool for changing their emotional states. You can also get the students' attention to begin the class by turning the music off. This can be a cue that it is now time to attend to other matters.

Music can also be used to stimulate movement or discussion. Play appropriate music in the background to make the students' actions more efficient. If the students are supposed to be moving about the room, play lively, upbeat music, and they will move to the faster tunes. If they are thinking or working by themselves, play soft baroque music in the background; this seems to help them remember more of what they are doing. If the students are working together in groups, play something soft in the background to minimize the intrusion one group can inflict upon another.

Properly employed, it [music] can create a heightened social learning context, motivate students to engage themselves more rapidly, and provide a sense of safety that might not otherwise be possible.

—Richard Allen (2002), *Impact Teaching*, p. 84

Although these are all good ways of incorporating music into your classroom as an accessory, you can also use music directly. Remember in the section on mnemonics where the students put difficult-to-remember rules, sequences, or formulas into rhymes? The same information can also be put to music. Start with a song with which all of the students are familiar, such as "If You're Happy and You Know It," and have the students set the new information to the same tune. If the majority of the class knows a song but one or two do not, the students who do know the song can teach it to the others. The songs are usually simple and catchy enough to learn easily. Conversely, the students who do not know the song can put the information to a song they know and teach that to the others. Doing both would actually be an immense boost to the students' memories.

32. Reading Strategies

When you speak to your children you use a different tone of voice and a different vocabulary—even a different rate of speaking—than that which you use when speaking with your boss. We subconsciously make many changes to adjust to our audiences and purposes when we speak to one another. The same must be true when we read. No matter what we read, we are reading for a purpose. We must keep this purpose in mind and change reading strategies accordingly. Those of us who are good readers do this without thought, but many students will need to be actively taught these strategies and when each strategy is appropriate. Allow the students to experiment with these strategies and discover which work best for them. Again, this is not an exhaustive list, but here are some common reading strategies your students could use:

- KWL Plus
- SQ3R
- PLAN
- Cornell note-taking

> Without adequate development of their schemata, they will stumble and falter instead of predicting and confirming with fluency. Furthermore, they'll read without meaning. . . . Without the proper schemata, people find it difficult or impossible to make inferences as they read.
>
> —Frank May (1982), *Reading as Communication*, p. 120

KWL Plus

KWL stands for Know, Want to Know, Learned. Before beginning to read about a particular topic, first have the students think about what they already know about it and list these things on a sheet of notepaper. Next, have them note what they would like to learn about the topic. Read the passage, and then have the students write what they have learned about the topic. The plus is summarizing what is read. When writing a summary, instruct the students to make a quick check of what they read, ensuring that the main points stay with them.

SQ3R: Survey, Question, Read, Recite, Review

Dating back to the early 1940s, SQ3R is now known as the grandfather of study strategies. Designed to be used with expository text, this strategy is best suited to textbook reading. Similar to KWL, SQ3R begins with a survey of the material about to be read. The student first flips through the chapter (or article), noting titles, headings, and captions to get an idea of what is about to be discussed. The student then writes down any questions that were generated by the preview and what he or she would like to learn on the topic. Next, the student reads the passage.

> Information that fits into or adds to an existing network has a much better chance of storage than information that doesn't.
>
> —Patricia Wolfe (2001), *Brain Matters: Translating Research Into Classroom Practice*, p. 97

While reading, he or she should periodically stop to reflect on what has been read, to interact with the text, and to answer self-generated questions. The student then reviews what he or she has learned and takes notes on the most important or relevant information.

PLAN: Predict, Locate, Add, and Note

This type of reading strategy makes use of graphic organizers: The students build a word map that helps them to understand what they will read. The graphic organizer used depends upon the reading the student is about to do. If it is all related to one subject, the student might want to use a web; if it is a comparison and contrast, a Venn diagram would be better; if sequential in time, a sequence chart. Whatever organizer is chosen, the student draws the chart, fills it in based on prior knowledge and prediction, and adds to it as the reading progresses. Finally, the student will note what he or she has learned. This, too, can come in many forms. Summarizing the article or redrawing and filling in the graphic organizer are two ways to review the material.

Cornell Note-Taking

Note-taking can be done in a few different ways. If the student has a real problem with reading comprehension, he or she might want to take short notes, jot down key words, or draw a picture of what is occurring in each paragraph. Alternatively, the student could wait until after the reading is completed. The Cornell note-taking strategy has the student divide a piece of paper into two sections, labeling one section "Main Points" and the other "Evidence/Details." The main points can come from reading the passage, or just from the subheadings of the passage. Recording the main points can be done after the reading is finished, or the student can jot these down as the reading progresses. The student will then fill in the other column with an explanation of what is in the first column.

> Personal or association connection is based on the association of past experience, past knowledge, or, in the event that there are no past experiences, on the associations that we create. It is the process of going from the known to the unknown.... Personal or association connection is the piece that gives ownership to the learning process. Prediction is another way we help create ownership to the learning by using students' natural curiosity to hook them into the learning.
>
> —Donna Walker Tileston (2005), *10 Best Teaching Practices*, p. 29

33. Field Trips

There are real-life, long-term benefits to taking field trips in class. Regardless of the type of field trip you are taking, field trips provide a positive break from the routine of the classroom. Field trips can be like the excursions you took in elementary school, where you did a lot of research before you went somewhere as a class, physically went there together, and spent a lot of time working on the topic when you got back. It might also mean having the students do visualization exercises. It could be getting out of the room to go outside, or even just switching rooms for the day. However, with current technology, it could also mean using the computer to explore parts of the world your students may never have an opportunity to visit. These are the four types of field trips that will be discussed here:

- excursions
- visualization
- change spaces
- virtual field trip

Excursions

Field trip excursions actually serve several purposes. Doing hands-on activities during the field trips has a positive impact on the students' abilities to recall information learned. The social impacts of field trips include teaching life skills and improving the social bonding among members of the class. The expeditions also help the students put the learned knowledge in context; they can link what they learned to the real-world application.

> Field trips provide students with real-world experiences that make the subsequent learning more understandable and memorable. In this new millennium, an additional option exists—to plan virtual field trips that carry students to places that would otherwise be inaccessible or cost prohibitive.
>
> —Marcia Tate (2003), *Worksheets Don't Grow Dendrites*, p. 15

Visualization

Visualization exercises aren't as powerful as field trips because they have the limitations of the students' experiences and imaginations. Students can't picture something they have never experienced. For instance, if a student has lived his whole life in the middle of Arizona and has never seen a picture of a lighthouse, asking him to visualize one on the ocean shore will not be successful. On the other hand, visualization can be powerful for vocabulary building, prewriting, or remembering facts. How you use visualization depends upon your purpose.

Recently my English as a Second Language class was reading a story that included the word *cupboard.* No one knew the meaning of the word. I explained that it was the place in the kitchen where you might put food or dishes. I told them to imagine that their kitchens had no storage areas and they decided to put in shelves. They attach a board to the wall and sit a cup on it. This is now the cup board. Add several more and put doors on them, and you have cupboards in your kitchen. This was a very logical explanation and an easy picture for them, but even difficult words can be remembered this way. If the mental pictures get ridiculous, it actually makes it easier to remember.

> Individuals can be taught to search their minds for images and be guided through the process to select appropriate images that, through hemispheric integration, enhance learning and increase retention.
>
> —David Sousa (2006), *How the Brain Learns (3rd ed.)*, p. 230

Often one of the most difficult phases of the writing process for students is getting started. Using visualization before they start writing can help to eliminate this frustration. Simply dim the lights before you start and have the students close their eyes. You might want to have soft baroque music playing in the background. Now walk them through an imaginary location step-by-step, telling them to look around and notice things, but do not describe anything for them. Ask them to smell the aromas, listen to the surrounding sounds, touch things, and maybe even taste things, but still refrain from describing anything. They are imagining this for themselves. Gently bring them back from their visualization into the present and ask them to write about what they saw, smelled, heard, felt, and tasted. You will be surprised at the detail you get in their writing.

A good reader creates mental pictures about the events that he or she is reading. However, people who have problems reading, especially problems with comprehension, often do not realize that is what you are supposed to do, nor do they know how to do it. When reading in class, stop every so often and discuss what you are reading, helping the students build their own mental pictures about what is going on. Have them put themselves in the place of a person about whom you are reading. If students can learn to do this type of visualization on their own, their reading comprehension will improve tremendously.

Changing Spaces

Changing the physical atmosphere of the class by going outside or even changing rooms with another teacher can activate the students' episodic memories. The context of the learning provides "invisible information" that is as much a part of the learning process as the content. However, be aware that the learning situation may have to be replicated to get recall. This means that the student may have to be in the same physical location to remember what was learned there.

> Many studies have been performed that prove that people who learn information in a specific location will remember that information better in the same location. (p. 80)
>
> Creating different atmospheres in your classroom can enhance the episodic memory lane. (p. 81)
>
> —Marilee Sprenger (2007), *Becoming a "Wiz" at Brain-Based Teaching*

Virtual Field Trips

Virtual field trips can be almost as meaningful as actual ones. They give the students the opportunity to experience different careers, cultures, countries, and an almost boundless list of learning prospects. With limited school funding and tightening restrictions, it is often impossible to take a class off campus to experience things. However, they can research the same things on the computer and bring the outside world into the school. There are also some great computer simulations that put the students in other situations and have them making decisions. These are especially prominent in history and are quite fun. PBS.org usually has one or two going on its Web site, but look around—there are many others available as well.

34. Discovery Learning

When I got my first computer I read two different manuals on how to run it. After reading them both cover to cover, I knew no more about how to run a computer than when I started, yet I still needed to be able to work my new computer. The way I actually learned to use my new computer was to get on it, mess around, and ask friends when I had specific questions. This is discovery learning.

In discovery learning the teacher suggests a learning objective, and the students work until they achieve it. Many students are able to learn more efficiently if they are able to work problems out for themselves.

For some students, though, discovery learning may put them in the frustration zone. These students require more direct instruction to build their skills before they are set free on the assignment (see "Scaffolding" later in this chapter).

Discovery learning can be an involved, ongoing project that lasts for weeks or months. However, it could also be something as simple as posting a series of pictures or problems around the room and having the students find the patterns, or having the students do a newspaper scavenger hunt, looking for specific things they might find in the newspaper.

However complex you choose to make the discovery learning process, remember that the students will all have different tolerances for frustration and that they will be able to process better if they can talk their way through it. Working in groups works great for this type of classroom design.

> In their book *Classroom Instruction That Works*, Robert Marzano, Debra Pickering, and Jane Pollock (2001) make three generalizations to discovery learning:
>
> 1. The discovery approach is difficult to use effectively when teaching skills.
> 2. When teachers use discovery learning, they should organize examples into categories that represent the different approaches to the skill.
> 3. Skills are most useful when learned to the level of automaticity. (pp. 137–140)

35. Cooperative Learning

The brain was built for survival. There are four primary modes of survival in which the brain engages: physiological, mental, emotional, and social. Students, from children to adults, must see school as related to these survival needs. If a student feels no sense of belonging in school, no sense of being involved, of caring or concern, that student will pay little attention to academic subjects. Even more overwhelming, the need for power is often largely ignored in the classroom. In using cooperative learning, these needs are satisfied. While working in groups, students begin to realize that they are members of a team. They have power within their teams and are important to the other members.

> Building a sense of teamwork and community strengthens the frontal lobes of the cortex and constructs roadways between the cortex, limbic system, and brain stem.
>
> —Becky Bailey (1998) *Brain Smart Teaching & Living*, p. 3

If school is to prepare students for the outside world, classes must be structured in ways that are congruent with the future lives of students. When students are employed, they will have to work with others; they will have to be responsible for one another, use social and communication skills, and use their knowledge and resources in collaborative activities with other people. In the working world each member of a team is responsible for his or her own work but is also judged on the performance of the group as a whole. In schools this is called cooperative learning, and it functions in exactly the same way.

> By structuring learning so that each student contributes to the group effort and is responsible for his or her own learning, one allows for individual accountability.
>
> —Gayle H. Gregory and Terence Parry (2006), *Designing Brain-Compatible Learning*, p. 120

36. Rituals

Rituals are comforting. People like to think they have a little control over their lives, and rituals offer this feeling of control and safety. Many of our students come from extremely unpredictable backgrounds that are full of stress. Beginning the day in class with rituals tells the students that this class is a safe place; these are people on whom they can rely.

> Classrooms need many rituals to provide this feeling of security, which may help de-stress the students.
>
> —Marilee Sprenger (2007), *Becoming a "Wiz" at Brain-Based Teaching*, p. 68

Of course, you will not be teaching each lesson in the same way or with the same materials. However, the use of the five-step lesson plan spoken of in this book can be a ritual in your class. The students will recognize where you are in the lesson and be able to anticipate the type of activity coming up. You can also use rituals in how you divide work, groups, and assignments. Think of things you do every day without much thought. Because people are such creatures of habit, you probably already have several rituals in your classroom without even realizing it. For example, in one of my classes, the students usually come in before I am in the room. When they enter the classroom they sign the attendance roster, answer the questions that are on the board, and write an entry in their journals. The beginning English as a Second Language class begins every day by writing the date on their slates, including the day of the week, what day yesterday was, and what day tomorrow will be. They end each class by doing pronunciation drills with each other, an exercise that they truly enjoy and always stay for. Doing a ritual at the beginning of class ensures that the students get there on time, because they don't want to miss out. Ending the class with a ritual keeps the students in class the whole time, because they know the class is going to end with a laugh. Imagine how many more rituals you can have in your class if you put your mind to creating them!

37. Novelty

Novelty can be used in a variety of ways. One can be novel in the approach used in the classroom, where the students sit, where the teacher stands, what the teacher wears, how the students are assessed—the list is almost endless. Although you want a fair amount of ritual in the classroom, you do not want so much that the class becomes boring.

There are four primary pathways to the memory: semantic, episodic, procedural, and emotional. (Some people also include automatic.) Using novelty in the classroom can help you to tap into all of them at the same time. For instance, one can wear different clothing or hats when talking of different topics; use props to emphasize the points; have the students sit in different seats, or on the floor or stand up during a minilecture; have the students read from a different source; or relate the information to an experience they once had. There are many, many ways to incorporate novelty in a classroom. Try some!

According to David Sousa (2006) in his book *How the Brain Learns (3rd ed.)*, using novelty simply means using a varied teaching approach that involves more student activity. He suggests using: humor, movement, multisensory instruction, quiz games, and music.

38. Art and Creativity

One way students can remember material is by drawing or creating with it. When students use art, they are able to visualize what they are learning, thereby using two more senses to move the learned material to memory (visual and kinesthetic). For some students, drawing something is the best way to remember it. It doesn't matter if anyone else understands the drawing, as long as the artist does.

Creativity can take forms other than drawing. The students can build dioramas of a scene; they can make a commercial for something you are studying; they can turn it into a poem or a song; they can make posters or collages; or they can write a story about it. However your students are talented, allow them to use their talents and be creative in representing what you are studying. By using their creativity, students are more likely to be able to apply the concepts to real life, and more likely to make the connections necessary to store what they have learned in long-term memory.

> What do you suppose would happen if that artistic ability, that spatial intelligence, were put to instructional use? How many vocabulary words could students actually acquire if they could illustrate the definitions rather than merely looking them up in the dictionary or glossary and writing down the first definitions they encounter? Brain and learning style theories support the idea that drawing strengthens memory, not only for vocabulary, but also for everything else.
>
> —Marcia Tate (2003), *Worksheets Don't Grow Dendrites*, p. 9

39. Scaffolding

Scaffolding is a way to provide additional support when the students need it, while still allowing them to discover and learn on their own. When you use scaffolding in lessons, you allow the students to work with what they know, until they come to the point that they need more assistance. You would then teach the next step or the next strategy and allow the students to practice with this new knowledge. There are a few things to keep in mind when using scaffolding with your students:

- To use scaffolding successfully, the instructor must first understand where the students' strengths and knowledge lie. If the students seem to be applying a certain strategy or skill to the exclusion of others, it is possible that they may need stronger scaffolds in other areas, or be reminded of other ways to do things.

- Teachers can provide extra support by giving the students verbal reminders as they are first practicing a new skill or strategy, gradually allowing the students more independence as they build confidence.

> In her book *Mastery Teaching*, Madeline Hunter (2004) asserts:
>
> First, we must determine which information is basic or essential to students' understanding of the content or process and then separate that information from information that may be desirable but is supplementary and can be acquired later. That basic information must be organized, so it becomes the scaffolding, or advance organizer, to which students can add more complex information. (p. 48)

- Choices and reminders can be posted around the room so that students can make decisions without having to ask explicit questions of the instructor.

- Students should evaluate their own work and how successful their approaches were, although they may need teacher guidance to do this.

- Once students are comfortable with a skill or strategy, have them apply it to a new context. The students may need more scaffolding as they attempt to modify what they know to fit the new application.

40. Manipulatives and Models

Manipulatives and models are not exactly the same thing, although they serve some of the same purposes. Manipulatives are items that can be touched and moved by students to introduce or reinforce a concept. They look nothing like what they are supposed to represent. We most often think of them as being used in math class, although they can certainly be used in other classes just as well. Models are more direct representations of something concrete, such as a skull or a building. They are often smaller than the actual item.

> The very act of generating a concrete representation establishes an image of the knowledge in students' minds.
>
> —Marzano, Pickering, and Pollock (2001), *Classroom Instruction That Works*, p. 78

Manipulatives are particularly useful in helping students move from the concrete to the more abstract levels of understanding. Before doing algebra, the students must really understand addition and subtraction. If the same students were to do their addition and subtraction with manipulatives, they are actually doing simple algebra. If the manipulatives were used in each step, as each new concept is introduced, the students would more easily grasp the new concepts and be able to adapt and modify them. Once the students understand with manipulatives, they can gradually be moved to the abstract. This can be done by using the same concepts and applying them to real situations at first, then moving to situations that are more theoretical.

The previous example was with math, but the same can be done with other subjects. Have students diagram sentences using different-colored tiles for each part of speech, find patterns in stories, or make connections in historical events. Manipulatives can be used in a variety of ways with diverse subjects.

Models differ from manipulatives only in that they look something like what they represent. Imagine a model of the solar system, or a seventeenth-century Pilgrim village. Although not exact miniatures of the original, one can easily visualize what the original might look like by looking at the model. If you use models to explain a concept to students, try leaving it prominently displayed in the classroom.

> I hear and I forget. I see and I remember. I do and I understand.
>
> —Confucius (551–479 B.C.)

Even if it isn't labeled or doesn't look particularly like the original (e.g., a wadded-up piece of paper representing the brain), seeing the model will help the students form a mental image of the original.

5

Debrief

Unfortunately, the debrief section is a part of the lesson plan that is often left out by teachers. However, this segment is essential for allowing the students to process information and to maintain it in long-term memory. During the debriefing, students are given the opportunity to practice what they have learned and check their learning with others. This section is a relatively short part of the lesson plan, lasting anywhere from 5 to 15 minutes. The teacher has a chance to clarify any points that may have been unclear to the students and link the new knowledge with what the students already knew.

One could easily adapt exercises from the "Engager" section of this book to use in debriefing; they have a lot in common. They are approximately the same length, and they are both designed to get the students talking about the subject matter.

The debrief section of the lesson plan doesn't have to be left to the very end of the class time. I debrief frequently throughout the lesson. If a class is an hour or two long, there will likely have been a lot of information disseminated by the end of the class time. Instead of waiting until the end, I find what I think are logical breaks in the information, or "chunks," and do a debriefing exercise for that portion of the lesson. I often do double duty with the debriefing exercise; it serves both as a debriefer and as an energizer. As with the engager, the time spent on this portion of the lesson is extremely flexible.

41. Up!

THIS ACTIVITY USES

- ■ visuals
- ■ wait time
- ■ writing

Objective

Students will briefly write answers on slates to check for understanding.

Time Required

Depends on the number of questions—about 30 seconds per question.

Materials

Each student will need a slate or dry-erase board and the corresponding supplies.

Procedure

1. Give each student the slate and equipment.
2. Ask a question that has a one-word or a numerical answer.
3. Instruct students to write the answers to the questions on their slates and hold them up.
4. After seeing who had the correct answers and who didn't, either tell the students the answer or write it on the board.
5. Ask another question.

Variations

- • You may allow the students to work together for the answers.
- • You may have the students take turns asking the questions.
- • You may also have the students work in pairs, asking one another questions.

EXAMPLE

As a way to check for understanding, the teacher of a geometry class says the names of shapes and angles. The students draw the shapes on their individual white boards. The teacher looks at all the boards to see who knew the answers and who didn't, then draws the correct shape on the board. No one but the teacher can see the students' answers, and the teacher now knows what the students need to work on more, and who needs extra practice.

Research for each of the elements that engage the brain in these debriefing exercises can be found with the energizers in Chapter 8, "Breaks and Energizers."

42. Board Races

THIS ACTIVITY USES

- competition
- movement
- social interaction
- time limit
- writing

Objective

Students will compete to write answers on the board.

Time Required

Time required depends on the subject and the number of participating students.

Materials

Chalkboard or dry-erase board.

Procedure

1. Have the students come to the board in pairs or some other small number (six or fewer).

2. Ask a question and have them write the answers on the board. Answers must be legible and spelled correctly.

3. The first one to turn around with the correct answer on the board gets to stay at the board. The rest will sit down and a new set of contestants will go to the board.

Variations

- Give slates to the students at their seats so that they can participate, even when they are not at the board.
- Divide the class into two to four teams and have the teams compete with one another.

EXAMPLE

During a literature class, the teacher divides the students into two teams. The first representative of each team goes to the board. The teacher asks a question pertaining to the plot or characters of the story they are reading. The students race to get the answer first, and turn around. The team gets the point if their representative turned around first and had the correct answer, spelled correctly. If that team's answer wasn't right, the teacher goes to the next team. If their answer was accurate and spelled properly, they get the point.

43. Hot Potato With a Twist

THIS ACTIVITY USES

- laughter
- movement
- novelty
- question development
- reviewing material
- social interaction
- time limit
- writing

Objective

Students will ask and answer questions while tossing an object to one another.

Time Required

30–45 seconds per question.

Materials

Small pieces of paper for students to make notes, an object to pass around, and a timer or music.

Procedure

1. Instruct the students to write questions on their note papers.
2. Have the students stand in a circle.
3. Instruct the student to pass the object around until the timer goes off or you stop the music.
4. When the timer goes off (or the music stops), the person holding the object gets to ask a question of the person who handed it to him.

Variations

- Half of their questions could pertain to the lesson just completed, the other half could be general.
- Have students toss the object to each other across the circle in a repetitive pattern.
- Use more than one object at a time.
- Have the students do this in small groups.

EXAMPLE

In a chemistry class, the teacher wanted to see how well the students knew the periodic tables. Rather than testing them or drilling them, the teacher elected to play hot potato. The students had fun asking each other the questions, and the teacher got the information he needed.

44. 7-Up With a Splash

THIS ACTIVITY USES

- movement
- novelty
- reviewing material
- social interaction

Objective

Students will secretly select other students, who must guess who touched them or answer a question.

Time Required

Usually 3–4 minutes per round.

Materials

None.

Procedure

1. Select seven students to be "it" (see Chapter 7, "How to Mix a Group"), and have them stand at the front of the room.

2. Instruct all other students to put their heads down on their desks (no peeking!) and one hand up in the air with the elbow resting on the desk. This hand should be in a loose fist with the thumb pointing up.

3. Those who are "it" will quietly circulate the room, each choosing one person and putting that person's thumb down.

4. After selecting their person, the "its" will return to the front of the room and say, "Heads up, seven up!"

5. Those who were chosen by having their thumbs put down will stand up. One by one, those who were chosen will try to guess who chose them. If they guess correctly, they get to be "it" for the next round, and take the other person's place. If not, they have to answer a question about the previously studied content.

Variation

- Before the game begins, have the students write the questions they will ask and then play the game until you are out of questions.

EXAMPLE

After studying the events leading to World War I, the class plays this game. When a student makes an incorrect guess, the teacher asks a question like: What countries made up the Central Powers? If the student answers incorrectly, the teacher asks if there are others who know it and confirms the correct answer, but the teacher only asks questions she thinks the student can answer.

45. Jeopardy

THIS ACTIVITY USES

- inferences
- question development
- reviewing material
- social interaction
- time limit
- writing

Objective

Students will recognize descriptions of content and be able to label it.

Time Required

Time required depends on the number of questions asked.

Materials

None.

Procedure

1. Have the students write questions and answers regarding the content just covered.
2. Divide the class into groups of two to four students (see Chapter 7, "How to Mix a Group").
3. Pose the "answer" of a question and give the students 30 seconds to confer on what the question might be. Instruct them to stand up when they think they know the question.
4. Call on the first group to stand and have them tell the question. If they get it wrong, call on the next.
5. The first group to get the right question gets the point.

Variations

- Give the students categories for which they need to write questions.
- Have the students write their questions in groups and write the name or the number of the group on the question so you don't ask the question of the authors.
- Don't have the groups stand; rather, take turns asking the groups to answer first.
- Everybody who got the right question gets a point.
- Have the groups write the questions on slates and hold them up.

EXAMPLE

After studying act one of *Romeo and Juliet*, the students are divided into groups. They are then instructed to write questions and answers about particular categories. For example, group one writes about characters, group two about plot, and so forth. With these questions, the class plays Jeopardy.

46. Bingo

THIS ACTIVITY USES

- rehearsal
- visuals

Objective

Students will play bingo as a review of content.

Time Required

2–3 minutes to fill out their cards; 7–10 minutes to play.

Materials

Chalkboard or dry-erase board, paper.

Procedure

1. Have the students fold their paper so that there are five squares going across, four down.

2. Instruct the students to write "BINGO" in the squares across the top of the paper.

3. Indicate to the students that they should write target words in each of the squares.

4. You may want to write the target words on the board for them, but put them on randomly so the students will mix them on their papers.

5. Play bingo.

Variation

- Instead of using place markers, have the students draw different geometric figures around the words each time you play or mark the words in different colors.

EXAMPLE

As a wrap-up to an algebra lesson, the teacher put all of the formulas on the board for the students to copy onto their bingo papers. Once they started playing the game, the teacher would call what the formula was for. For example, the teacher would say: The area of a triangle. The students would mark: 1/2bh. In this way, the students were getting practice recognizing the formulas, and the teacher could tell who didn't know the formulas.

47. Cartoons

THIS ACTIVITY USES

- art
- novelty
- summarizing

Objective

Students will draw what they have learned.

Time Required

5–15 minutes.

Materials

Paper and pencil for each student, perhaps colored pencils or crayons.

Procedure

1. Instruct the students to draw the most important things they have learned in the lesson. Remind them that their artistic talent is not being judged; you just want them to be able to represent their learning.

2. Each student should show their drawing to at least one other person and explain its significance.

Variations

- Give the students paper with "windowpanes" on it (boxes for the cartoons) and have them draw a series of cartoons.
- Divide the students into groups and have the students of each group work only on specific aspects of the lesson.

EXAMPLE

To see if the students understood the plot of the story being read in literature class, the teacher had them draw the events as though they were a cartoon. If they left out something important or put in things that were unimportant, the teacher would know she needed to work on it a bit more.

48. Each One, Teach Three

THIS ACTIVITY USES

- movement
- rehearsal
- social interaction
- summarization
- vocalization

Objective

Students will teach something to three other people.

Time Required

5 minutes.

Materials

A 3 × 5 note card for each student.

Procedure

1. Instruct the students to write one thing on their note cards that they want to be able to remember from the lesson.

2. Ask each student to teach the item to at least three other people. They will teach it by telling other students the item, the other person will repeat it, and then the first person will repeat it again. For example,

   "Did you know that the U.S. government has three branches?

   "The U.S. government has three branches?"

   "Yes, the U.S. government has three branches."

3. When they have taught three people their information, they should continue until time is up. (Hint: don't give too much time, or students will get off task.)

Variations

- Students can write as many as three items to teach.
- Students can teach their items to a preassigned set of students.

EXAMPLE

When studying the aforementioned government lesson, the students will write down the one thing they are having the most trouble remembering. After having repeated it so many times, they will remember the fact. Furthermore, they will be hearing facts from the other students, giving them even more chances of learning.

49. Schema Mapping

THIS ACTIVITY USES

- comparing
- cooperative learning
- finding patterns and connections
- visuals

Objective

Students will arrange the newly learned information into various types of graphic organizers.

Time Required

5–15 minutes.

Materials

None.

Procedure

1. Choose an appropriate graphic organizer (see "Graphic Organizers" in Chapter 4, "Activities").

2. Model how to use the graphic organizer.

3. Divide the students into pairs or groups of three (see Chapter 7, "How to Mix a Group").

4. Have the groups put what they have just learned into the graphic organizer.

Variations

- Have the groups meet with other groups to compare the graphic organizers and note any differences.
- Draw a "master" graphic organizer, incorporating everyone's work.

EXAMPLE

While reading a book in class, the student groups each chose characters to follow. At the end of each chapter, the groups followed their character through the elements of the plot, stating what his or her role was and adding this information to the graph they were making as they went.

50. Turn to Your Neighbor

THIS ACTIVITY USES

- reviewing material
- social interaction
- summarization
- vocalization

Objective

Students will recap the lesson to one another.

Time Required

2–5 minutes.

Materials

None.

Procedure

1. Predetermine who will act as "neighbors" to one another.

2. After teaching a lesson, or a portion of a lesson, ask the students to turn to their neighbors and reteach what they have just learned.

Variations

- Have the students choose new "neighbors" after they have met with the first.
- Provide models for the students to use when teaching.

EXAMPLE

After the teacher finished explaining the parts of the atom, the students explain the atom to each other.

51. Interview the Expert

THIS ACTIVITY USES

- ■ movement
- ■ novelty
- ■ question development

- ■ social interaction
- ■ summarization
- ■ vocalization

Objective

Students will interview one another as though they were reporters finding out something new.

Time Required

5–10 minutes.

Materials

None.

Procedure

1. Ask the students to make a list of questions to use for interviewing an expert on the subject covered.

2. Pair the students. Assign one of each pair the role of "interviewer," the other the role of "expert." Give them a set amount of time to interview. (Probably no more than 2–3 minutes.)

3. When time is up, have the students switch roles. Give them slightly less time for the second interview.

Variations

- • Have the interviewers write the answers down.
- • Change the topic a bit for the second interview.
- • Videotape the interviews.

EXAMPLE

After finishing a lesson on government, the students write their interview questions. They can look something like this:

Who makes up the legislative body of the government?

What does this branch do?

Who are the representatives from our area in the legislative branch?

For how long are they elected?

It doesn't matter if both interviewers in the pair have some of the same questions.

52. Alphabet Summaries

THIS ACTIVITY USES

- finding patterns and connections
- social interaction
- summarizing
- vocalization

Objective

Students will write important points from the lesson that begin with each letter of the alphabet.

Time Required

5–15 minutes.

Materials

Paper for each group of students.

Procedure

1. Have the students write the alphabet down the left-hand side of the page, one letter on every other line.

2. In groups of two to four people, have the students write summarizing statements beginning with each letter.

3. As a class, make a master list on the board of the statements of the groups.

Variations

- Have the groups confer with one another to develop their own master lists.
- Divide the alphabet so that each group is only working with a few letters.

EXAMPLE

After finishing the unit on the Civil War, the class divides into groups. The groups write the point of the war on the chart. Expect each group to have different points. Their chart will look something like this:

A—Artillery	Most artillery was made in the north. Soldiers made their own bullets.
B—Bull Run	The first major battle of the Civil War
C—Confederates	People from the southern states that seceded from the Union

53. Bumper Stickers

THIS ACTIVITY USES

- art
- cooperative learning
- novelty
- social interaction
- summarization

Objective

Students will summarize the content of the lesson into short statements that would fit on a bumper sticker.

Time Required

About 5 minutes to write, more to share.

Materials

Three to five strips of construction paper, approximately four inches by eight inches, for each pair of students; crayons or markers.

Procedure

1. Divide the students into pairs.

2. Pass out construction paper and markers or crayons.

3. Have students work together to find short, summarizing statements for the major points of the lesson. They may want to make the bumper stickers artistic.

4. Ask the students to share their bumper stickers and explain the significance of each.

Variation

- Display the bumper stickers and ask the other students to figure out the significance of them.

EXAMPLE

After studying China, the students make bumper stickers that summarize the lessons. The slogans could be something like this:

China: The Oldest Country in the World

Long before Pink Floyd, there was The Wall.

If you like paper, the compass, gunpowder, or printing, thank the Chinese.

54. Newsbreak!

THIS ACTIVITY USES

- cooperative learning
- novelty
- social interaction
- summarization
- vocalization

Objective

Students will design short news segments to explain what they have learned.

Time Required

5 minutes to write the news segments; about 10 minutes to report.

Materials

None.

Procedure

1. Divide the class into pairs or groups of three.
2. Tell the students that they are going to make 30-second news bulletins.
3. Give the students 5 minutes to summarize what they learned from the previous lesson into a 30-second blurb like the ones they would see on TV in the evenings.
4. After the time is up, have the different groups "report the news."
5. Discuss the differences in the reports—that is, what was seen as important for one group versus what another group saw as important.

Variations

- Change the amount of time the newscasts last. For example, have them last for only 15 seconds instead of 30.
- Have some of the students videotape their newscasts and use them for review.

EXAMPLE

When studying the Vietnam War, the students could feel as if they were there if they were reporting on it:

This is a CBS News Break. The conflict in Vietnam continues to expand as the United States drafts more boys to fight. As of today, December 30, 1965, there are 184,000 American troops in Indochina. This is the most unpopular war in the century, but U.S. leaders appear to remain unresponsive to widespread protests here at home. There will be more on this later tonight, on the 11:00 Nightly News.

55. Top Ten

THIS ACTIVITY USES

- social interaction
- summarization

Objective

Students will complete a list, ranking what they have learned.

Time Required

5–10 minutes.

Materials

None.

Procedure

1. Divide the students into pairs or groups of three.

2. Instruct the groups to make a list of the ten most important aspects of the lesson, starting with the least important (number 10) and ending with the most important (number 1).

Variation

- Groups could make smaller lists, then, as a class or in larger groups, the students could get together and compare their answers, incorporating all of the ideas but ranking them with values.

EXAMPLE

The ten most important things about the lesson on the circulatory system are:

1. Pacemakers can help regulate heart rate.
2. Blood pressure is the amount of force exerted by the blood on the walls of the arteries.
3. Exercise increases the heart rate.
4. The healthier the heart, the slower the beat (usually between 60 and 100 beats per minute for adults).
5. Veins return deoxygenated blood to the heart.
6. Arteries take oxygenated blood to the tissues.
7. Blood vessels consist of arteries, capillaries, and veins.
8. The circulatory system consists of the heart, blood, and blood vessels.
9. The circulatory system helps stabilize body temperature.
10. The circulatory system moves substances to and from the cells.

56. Hot Dog

THIS ACTIVITY USES

- competition
- laughter
- movement
- novelty
- social interaction
- time limit

Objective

Students will compete to answer questions.

Time Required

5–15 minutes.

Materials

Small stuffed animal (mine is a dog) and low stool or desk.

Procedure

1. Divide the class into two groups.
2. Set the stuffed animal on the desk or stool in the front of the room.
3. Have a representative from each group go to the front of the room and stand on either side of the stuffed animal; not touching it, but within arm's reach. (They should put their hands behind their backs.)
4. Ask a question that has a one-word or short answer.
5. The one who grabs the stuffed animal first gets to answer the question. If the answer is correct, the other person sits down and a new representative from that group comes to the front. If the first person to get the stuffed animal guesses the wrong answer, the other one gets to try. If the second guesser gets the correct answer, the first one sits down and is replaced by a new representative. If neither is correct, they are both replaced.

Variations

- Have the students write the questions.
- Have the students write and ask the questions.

EXAMPLE

When learning to edit sentences for grammar, each team sends a representative to the board, and they prepare to play the game. The teacher reads a sentence such as, "The children was in the garage." The students compete to get the toy. The one who grabs the toy first gets to answer the question. If that student gives the wrong answer, the other student gets to guess. Whoever doesn't get a point sits down, and a new person from that team comes up.

57. Give Them the Finger

THIS ACTIVITY USES

- building community
- metacognition
- social interaction

Objective

Students will rate the difficulty level of the activity and discuss their thoughts.

Time Required

1–3 minutes.

Materials

None.

Procedure

1. First, the teacher must explain and model what the students are about to do.

2. Divide the class into groups of four to six students.

3. Tell the students that they are going to rank the difficulty level of the previous activity from one to five (one being very easy, five being very difficult).

4. The teacher will count slowly to three, and at "three" the students will all hold out, on their fingers, how they ranked the activity in difficulty.

5. If there is more than a one-point difference within the group, they should talk about the parts of the lesson they thought were difficult and why.

Variations

- The groups could report to the class what they discussed.
- This could also be done as a whole class instead of in groups.

EXAMPLE

After having read a poem in class and briefly discussed it, the students get into their groups and rank their understanding.

58. Circle Stories

THIS ACTIVITY USES

- imagination
- social interaction
- summarization

Objective

Students will work together to give a summary of the lesson.

Time Required

Time required depends on the number of participating students and how many summarizing sentences you want to have.

Materials

None.

Procedure

1. Have all the students stand or sit in a large circle.

2. Tell them that they are going to work together to summarize a lesson, one word at a time.

3. Start the sentence with one word, preferably the topic for the lesson.

4. Instruct the student to your left to add a word.

5. Continue around the circle, each student adding only one word at a time, until they have all developed a summary.

Variations

- This can also be done sentence-by-sentence, rather than word-by-word.
- The exercise can go around the circle only once or can continue until you are satisfied with the summary.

EXAMPLE

After studying the life cycle of plants, the teacher begins the review exercise by saying, "Plants . . ." The students add to the sentence, one word at a time, describing the life cycle.

59. Concentration

THIS ACTIVITY USES

- finding patterns and connections
- rehearsal
- social interaction

Objective

Students will match cards.

Time Required

Time required depends on the number of words you want to cover.

Materials

Thick paper cut into equivalent rectangles, approximately two inches by four inches, and writing utensils.

Procedure

1. Divide the students into pairs.

2. Have each student write the target words he or she should know on the rectangular papers.

3. Tell the pairs to mix their cards together, and then lay them all face down on the floor or on a desk.

4. Each student can turn over two cards each time it's his or her turn, reading each out loud. If the cards match, the student gets to keep them; if they don't match, the student must put the cards back where they were found.

5. The one with the most matching cards wins.

Variations

- Students can draw pictures on one card, words on the matching ones.
- Students can write the word on one card, the definitions on the matching ones.

EXAMPLE

To review vocabulary, the students write the target words on one card, a synonym or brief definition on the other. They then play Concentration with their cards.

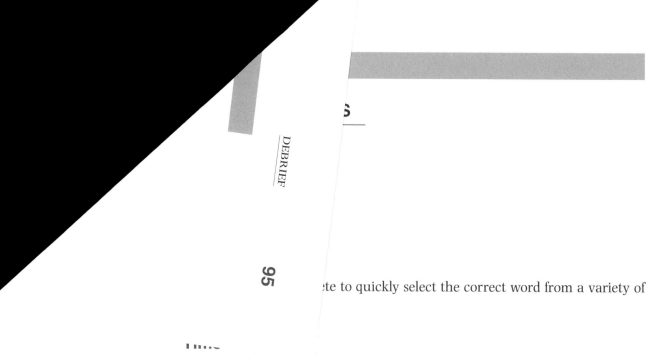

...te to quickly select the correct word from a variety of

Time

5–10 minutes.

Materials

Chalkboard or dry-erase board or an overhead projector, or both.

Procedure

1. Divide the class into two teams.

2. Write a variety of words on the overhead or chalkboard. The words should not be in any order or even on the board linearly. (Hint: this really works better if the words are written on a transparency and shone on the board. If they are written directly on the board, they will rub off during the course of the game.)

3. Each team sends a representative to the board, who will get a flyswatter.

4. The teacher will give a definition or read a clue. The first person to hit the appropriate word with the flyswatter wins the round. The other person will sit down and that team will send a new representative to the board.

Variations

- You could have both participants sit down so that the whole class gets a chance to play.
- You could also include words on the board that don't pertain to the lesson.

EXAMPLE

After the lesson in economics, the teacher puts all of the vocabulary words on the board that the class has had so far. The words are not in any order but scattered all over. After dividing the class, one person from each group goes to the board. The teacher reads the definition of a word, and the students race to hit the correct word with the flyswatter.

6

Story and Metaphor

This section of the lesson plan does not take long, only 2–5 minutes, but it is extremely important in ensuring that the students can fit their new knowledge into their existing schemata. This means that the students need to be able to process the knowledge with their current understandings of the world. Each person has a unique way of viewing the surrounding world. For new knowledge to be stored in the brain, the student must be able to make this information fit in with what he or she already knows. Think of it this way: If you travel to work every day by the same route and one of the roads is suddenly closed, to find an alternate route you will need to use what you already know about the commute. You won't have to find out anew the direction and distance you need to travel, but you will need to find out about different streets or highways. Once you know alternative routes, you combine that information with what you already know about how to get to work. Voilà! You have a new way to go to work!

> In his book *How the Brain Learns (3rd ed.),* David Sousa (2006) states that "metaphors are usually rich in imagery, are useful bridging strategies, and can apply to both content and skill learning." (p. 161)

Using stories and metaphors works the same way with your students. Your students have an active way of looking at the world, and any new knowledge

In her book *Learning Structures,* Ruby Payne (2001, p. 7) states that "when mental models are directly taught, abstract information can be learned much more quickly because the mind has a way to contain it or hold it." To discover students' mental models, ask them to sketch or tell an analogy, story, or metaphor.

will have to somehow be made to fit with what they already know. Supplying them with mental models helps to guide them through the process of linking the new with the existing.

Mental models can come in two different modes: Tell a story about how this knowledge directly fits into their lives or their current study, or make an analogy to something completely unrelated. In this chapter, I chose an analogy: finding a new way to travel to work.

EXAMPLE

When teaching about negative and positive numbers, the teacher relates it to money. Every time the student sees a negative number it means, "I owe money." Every time the student sees a positive number, it means, "Someone paid me money." Therefore, $-4 - 5$ means, "You owed me four dollars, then borrowed five more." -4×6 means, "You owed four dollars to six different people."

7

How to Mix a Group

There are many ways in which one might mix a group, and it is rarely important how it is done. The following are just a few examples.

61. Playing Cards: Color (Two Groups)

Make sure that you have an equal number of red and black cards out, and only the number of cards you need, so that you have one for each student. Shuffle the cards you will use and hand them out randomly. To divide the class in half, have those with red cards stand on one side of the room, with black on the other.

62. Playing Cards: Suit (Four Groups)

Make sure that you have only the number of cards out for the number of students you anticipate. Also, when you separate the cards, get all the cards of each rank, or as close to all as you need. For instance, if you have twelve students you may want to use all the nines, tens, and jacks. Shuffle the cards you will use and hand them out randomly. Divide the class by suit (e.g., all the hearts in one corner, the clubs in another).

63. Playing Cards: Number

Again, make sure that you have only the number of cards out for the number of students who will be participating. How you separate the cards by rank depends on the sizes of groups you want. If you want two in a group, use two of each rank, three for three in a group, and so forth. Shuffle the cards you will use and hand them out randomly. Have the students find the others with the same rank on their cards.

64. Playing Cards: Number and Color

You can also create pairs when you had originally passed out the cards to create groups of four. Divide the cards and pass them out as before. To divide the class into pairs, separate the students by number, and then again by color (e.g., black nines are together, red nines are together).

65. Birthday Line Up

Have the students line up according to their birthdays: January 1 at the front of the line and December 31 at the end of the line. You can then just count off the number of students you want in each group.

66. Birthday Week

If you want four groups, you can have the students divided according to the week of their birthday (e.g., the first 7 days of the month, the second 7 days, etc.). You can do the same if you want only two groups by placing those born in the first part of the month on one side of the room and those born in the last part of the month on the other side.

67. Numbered Craft Sticks

This is perhaps the easiest way to divide the students. Write a number on one end of each stick, corresponding to the number of students in the class. The number will match with each student when the students are listed in alphabetical order. Put the stick, number down, in a jar or vase. When you want to form groups, simply randomly pull the appropriate number of sticks for each member of the group and read the number on the stick. If the students don't know where they are in alphabetical order, make sure you have the list handy to advise them of their groups.

68. Color of Clothing

Choose any piece of clothing to use to divide the class. For instance, separate those with and those without shoestrings to be on different teams, as well as those with predominantly red in their shirts, or blue, white, and so forth. Although it is often more difficult to get groups with exactly the same numbers using this method, it is almost always random, and the groups will consist of different students every day.

69. Volunteers

When asking for volunteers, you don't always have to select the persons who raise their hands. Think of selecting the person on the volunteer's left, or everyone wearing the same color of shoes as the volunteer.

70. Physical Attributes

While dividing the class according to physical attributes can be very effective, it can also be dangerous. You can, perhaps, separate the class by the length of hair, or size of foot, but there are few other ways it can be done without dividing the class according to race or ethnic group. It is probably best just to stay away from this one altogether, unless you have a group that is extremely homogenous.

71. Hobbies

There are several ways to use hobbies as a separator. This works best if you know your audience well. You may use the last genre of book read, the last type of game played, favorite game, and so forth.

72. Collections

As with hobbies, a class can be divided by the things the participants collect or would like to collect. You may want to ask for suggestions from the class, or just come up with your own ideas of collectibles.

73. Last Number of Phone Number

It is probably best to use the last number because it is the least confusing. Of course, other numbers can be used, but phone numbers seem to be the least invasive. By using the numbers, you can divide the class into two groups (1–5, 6–0), or up to 10 groups. If someone does not have a phone, have him or her use another number.

74. Last Letter of Name

Using the last letter seems to mix the group a little better than using the first letter does. You can also choose to use the second or third letter of the student's name. This works equally well regardless of whether you use the first name or the last. Be aware, though, that some cultures do not use middle names, so you may want to steer away from using them as your mixer. Also, many languages use the family name first and the given name last. Be clear which name you are intending for them to use, if you care which.

75. Four Corners

This was also mentioned in the activities part of the lesson plan. Use this to divide the class by asking opinion questions on something fairly noncontroversial like fashion, favorite television show, music, or pet (i.e., those preferring cats on one side of the room, dog people are on the other side, others are in the middle).

76. Picture Match

Have pairs of pictures and give one to each student (you can download them from the Internet). One of the pictures should be an obvious match for the other. For instance, a broom and dustpan, mop and bucket, baseball and glove, and so forth. This will put the students in pairs. If you want to put them in larger groups, make several of them repeats (e.g., three brooms and three dustpans will make a group of six).

77. Proverbs

Find sufficient proverbs so that there are enough for half of the class. Give the first half of the proverb to half of the students, the last half to the other students and have them find their matches. For instance, "A stitch in time," may be the first half, and "saves nine" the second half. Again, this works to make pairs, unless you have more than one of the same proverb.

78. Opposites

Randomly give students small pieces of paper with words that are natural opposites of one another. For example, one student will have *black*, another *white*. One student will have *sit* another *stand*.

79. Synonyms

Randomly give students small pieces of paper with words that are synonyms of one another. For example, one student will have *house*, another will have *home*. One student will have *lamp*, another will have *light*.

80. Categories

If you want larger groups, give words that fall into the same category to the appropriate number of students. For instance, if you want groups of four, randomly pass out words like: *mittens, coat, scarf,* and *hat*. Another group might have words like: *sand, water, sun,* and *lotion*. The first task the students will have as a group is to name their category.

8

Breaks and Energizers

> Receiving constant input is not as effective as receiving input punctuated by breaks for processing the input. It is not helpful to pour more water into a cup that is already full. Reflection time reinforces the neural connections that are created through learning. Give students frequent breaks in reading, videos, lectures, filmstrips to process what they've learned.
>
> —Kagan Cooperative Learning (2001), *Kagan SmartCards*,
> taken from the "Brain-Based Learning" card

Time spent *not* learning new content is extremely important because this is when the brain processes the new information. We cannot learn unlimited amounts of explicit content, so overloading your students' brains by covering more material is destructive. The amount of time a brain can spend taking in new information has many variables: age, maturity, amount of sleep, nutrition, and so forth. Generally, for adults and older teens, every 17–22 minutes the students will need to change gears. After this amount of time, the students will drift off. The brain can attend to something for only so long, and then it will take a short vacation. If the instructor schedules and directs the breaks, he or she can ensure how long the breaks will be and that the learners will return from their mental vacations. Otherwise, when the students take their mental breaks, and when (or if) they return from them, is totally in the control of the learners.

Movement will increase energy levels, improve storage and retrieval of information, and dopamine levels (therefore, overall good feelings). A short break or energizer increases arousal. Movement is a basic necessity for the brain. Mainly, you want the students to have an opportunity to stand up and move around. They need to get their blood flowing so that their brains are better oxygenated, and consequently, better fed. The breaks need to last only a couple of minutes. The following are a few suggestions; eventually, you will think of many of your own, and your students will make suggestions.

81. Foot/Arm Spin

Have the students stick their right feet out and turn them in a clockwise direction. Next, tell them to hold their left arms in front of them and turn them in a counterclockwise direction while still turning their feet. You may alternate hands and feet, but keep them going in the opposite directions. This gets easier with practice, but is almost impossible at first. This activity is a cross-lateral (i.e., it involves both sides of the brain) and so is great for brain stimulation.

82. Same/Different Pictures

Randomly pass out pictures that are similar but have some differences. First, have the students find who has the match to their pictures. Then have them find what the differences are. This activity allows for social interaction and problem solving.

83. Indoor Volleyball

This is not actually volleyball; it is just tossing balls around the room. You can do this with just one beach ball, or you can use several. If you use more than one ball, it is good to have more than one size (the brain has to adjust for weight and mass when deciding how hard and how high to hit the ball), but the balls should all be very light so that they are easy to keep in the air. Have all the students stand up and then toss the ball at someone, telling them that the only rule is that the ball can't touch the floor. If you notice some areas that are not getting any action, simply call out, "Hit it to the corners" or "Send it to someone in red." Try to make sure that everyone has an opportunity to hit the ball. This allows for both movement and fun.

84. Name Game

This is great for big groups or groups that do not know one another well. Have all the students stand in a large circle. Throw the ball to someone on the opposite side of the circle and ask that person what his or her name is. When that person answers, tell him or her to do likewise—toss the ball to someone on the opposite side and ask his or her name. Keep going around the circle until everyone has had the ball. Next, do it again, but this time call out the person's name as you toss the ball to him or her. Speed up the process a bit. After they get comfortable with this, you can do a couple of things. Turn the process around: Have students throwing the ball to the person from whom they had originally received it. Alternatively, introduce a variety of balls of different shapes, weights, and sizes. (I even use some beanbags.) These get going quite fast, and it really forces the students to react, while doing several things with their brains at once, and thus activating both sides of it. It also allows for movement and social interaction.

The Name Game came from Kim Bevill (2004), who used it in a presentation at a Brain Expo Conference.

---

85. Isometrics

In isometrics, a force is applied to an immovable object. There are several ways to do isometrics in class: Have the students put their hands together as though praying and push the hands against one another; have the students do standing push-ups against a wall; or have them hold a book, with both hands, behind their head and then lift it over their head. However you choose to do it, isometrics, like any other type of exercise, increases blood flow to the muscles and releases tension. You may want to couch this with some deep-breathing relaxation as well.

86. Simon Says

This is the same game you played as a child. To promote movement and social interaction, the leader gives the instructions, and if he or she includes the phrase "Simon Says" at the beginning of the command, the class follows. Nobody is ever "out" of the game and sitting down. Let the students take turns leading the game.

87. Hand Slap

Have the students kneel on hands and knees, forming a circle. Each student crosses forearms with his or her neighbor. Tell one person to slap the ground and have the slap continue around the circle—in order of the hands, not the people. Any person may change the direction of the slap by slapping twice. When someone makes a mistake, the direction of the hand-slapping changes. Watch out! This is actually much harder than it sounds, but the brain loves to find patterns.

88. Jumping Jacks

Have students do a few jumping jacks or march around the room moving their arms for a couple of minutes. Movement is good in the classroom.

89. Crisscross

To promote cross-laterals, have student touch their left hand to their right knee, and right hand to their left knee, as slowly as possible. Very gradually speed up the process.

90. Follow the Leader

This is just like the game you played as a child. Designate a student to be the leader and allow him or her to lead for a certain amount of time (30 seconds or so). Make sure you eventually let all of the students lead (not necessarily in the same day). This is best done to music so the brain can match the movements to the rhythm. Their brains will be finding patterns while the body is moving.

91. Line Dancing

There are actually several ways you could do this. You could do this as a whole class or in groups. You could show students a simple dance or have them make their own. The dances should be simple and, preferably, involve some crossover movements. The brain is finding patterns, and this allows for both movement and social interaction.

92. Stretching

Simply having the students stand up and stretch increases cerebrospinal fluid flow to the brain and blood oxygenation.

93. Toss Across

To promote social interaction and movement, have groups of two start by throwing something to each other (ball, beanbag, etc.). They start very close together. Each time one of them catches the ball without dropping it, the catcher takes a step backward. If they miss, they have to return to where they started.

94. Juggling

Start out by using scarves, gradually working your way up to beanbags or balls. Starting with scarves allows the brain to learn the movements slowly, so that they are automatic when moving up to the faster-falling objects. The cross-lateral movements are great for getting brains "unstuck" by involving both hemispheres.

95. Jacks

Get several sets of jacks and have the students play for a couple of minutes. This allows for visuals, social interaction and movement. Do not let them sit at their desks to play; make them move!

96. Gotcha!

Have all the students stand in a large circle holding their left arm out to their sides, palms up, and their right hands out, index finger pointing down. Each person should have a right finger pointing about two inches above the neighbor's left hand. Tell them, "When I say go, try to capture that person's finger with your right hand, but don't let the other person get your finger!" After they have tried this a couple of times, have them take one step forward, cross their arms in front of them, and try it again. This cross-lateral game is really fun and great to play when everyone is tired.

Gotcha! also came from Kim Bevill (2004) of Columbine, Colorado.

97. Rhythm

Have all the students stand and one student lead the group. The leader will develop a rhythm using a combination of hand claps, slaps on the legs, finger snaps, and so forth. The leader should start slowly, with only a few motions, and make the rhythm more difficult as they go. When the students seem to have trouble keeping up, change to a new leader. This allows for both pattern finding and movement.

98. Kick the Can—Desk Style

The students form groups of four to six and gather around a desk or table. They start with a small paper wad (use half a sheet) and flip (with forefinger and thumb) the paper wad to someone else. The goal is to see how long they can keep the paper moving without touching it (except with those two fingers) and without letting it drop off the desk. This allows for social interaction and movement.

99. Silent Ball

All students sit on their desks. Start with a small, soft ball. The students throw the ball to one another until someone fails to catch it. The person who was supposed to catch it is out and sits on the floor. If the ones on the floor are able to catch a ball without getting up, they are back in and may get back on their desks. (Of course, the one for whom the ball was intended is now out.) The last one to be on the desk wins. Again, this allows for social interaction and movement. Once the students get pretty good at the game, try adding a second ball.

100. Have a Ball!

Have each student write his or her name on a piece of paper and wad it up. Tell them to throw the paper wads to the opposite side of the room. Now each person should find a paper wad and pick it up. Upon reading the name on the paper, they should find that person and ask them a question. This promotes the building of community and allows for both social interaction and movement.

Appendix A

Lesson Plan Samples

This appendix begins with a reminder of the components of the five-part model for lesson plans. Following this is a blank outline that you can copy and use for your own plans and examples of what lesson plans might look like when some of the activities from this book are incorporated into your teaching. Remember that this plan is meant to be extremely flexible so that it fits what, whom, and when you are teaching. The times listed are only suggestions and will need to be modified to accommodate your lessons. Insert the brain breaks whenever you feel your students start to drift or need to be energized.

The Five-Part Model for Lesson Plans

■ 1. ENGAGER ⏱ (2–5 MINUTES)

Used to engage the students' attention, this is deliberately inserted into the lesson to help prepare the students for learning. It is a brief activity to cause a change of state in the students and help them to mentally leave their "baggage" behind. This step helps the instructor to quickly grab the attention of the learners, and helps students to fully attend to the situation at hand.

■ 2. FRAME ☐ (<1 MINUTE)

Used to create an appropriate perspective, this section of the lesson plan helps the learner to answer the questions: Why should I attend to this topic? What will it matter to me? The frame should be at the beginning of the lesson so that the students have a reason to pay attention.

■ 3. ACTIVITY (5–30 MINUTES)

Note that the root word to this is *active*. To bring about a conceptual awareness, the experience introduces the basic ideas or concepts being taught. Learning should be an active process: mentally, kinesthetically, socially, emotionally, or some combination of these. It should be a creative process in conjunction with some instruction apart from lecture.

■ 4. DEBRIEF (5–15 MINUTES)

This is the component of the lesson in which the teaching points are highlighted or clarified. The students discover and integrate key aspects of the activity for themselves. The experience and conversation are narrowed down to the key points, making sure that everyone understands to meanings of the activity.

■ 5. STORY AND METAPHOR (2–5 MINUTES)

This is where the instructor ensures that the material is made "real" to the student by including a story, metaphor, or other device. This gives the students something to "hang their hats on." It also helps them to view the information from a broader perspective.

THE FIVE-PART MODEL FOR LESSON PLAN ■

Language Arts: Reading

Topic:

A look at the characters in the novel *To Kill a Mockingbird*, by Harper Lee

Engager:

Interview: Man on the Street. Students interview one another as a reminder of what has happened in the last chapter the class read.

Frame:

Stories help us to understand the world around us and how it functions. If we can learn to understand characters in stories and their motivations, we will be more capable of understanding the people around us and why they do some of the things they do.

Activity:

Divide the class into groups of three to five students, one group per character. Each group is assigned a character and must make a graphic organizer for him or her, defining the character's role in the plot of the story.

Debrief:

The students design questions and answers about their character to be used in playing Jeopardy. They will stay in their groups for the game, but the group will not be allowed to answer questions about their own character during the game.

Metaphor:

Trying to understand people and why they do some of the things they do is like trying to solve a crossword puzzle when some of the clues are in a foreign language. Some of the time you might be able to figure it out by looking at what else is going on, but sometimes you just have to move on and hope it makes sense later.

■ THE FIVE-PART MODEL FOR LESSON PLAN

Science

Topic:

The causes of earthquakes and volcanoes

Engager:

Play Reporter Relay with a picture of a city that has been hit by an earthquake.

Frame:

The more we know about the causes of earthquakes, the more likely it will be that some day we will be able to predict them.

Activity:

After having studied the layers and plates of the earth, divide the class into pairs and instruct them to draw and label the different layers of the earth. Next, give the groups six different colors of clay and have them create models of the earth, keeping in mind that colors represent temperature and that the crust has fissures.

Debrief:

Once the models are made, have the students cut them in half, each taking a half with them. Instruct the students that they are each to teach three people about their model.

Metaphor:

The earth is like a pimple; you don't really think about what's going on beneath the surface until it erupts.

THE FIVE-PART MODEL FOR LESSON PLAN   ■

Economics

Topic:

Check-cashing stores

Engager:

Play Do You Know Your Neighbor. End the game with statements like, "I have a neighbor who borrows money every week." Whether anyone changes or not, you can use this to lead into the frame.

Frame:

Some things happen so gradually that you don't notice the impact unless you sit back and really look at it. Today we are going to look at the real costs of getting the money for your paycheck before payday.

Activity:

This activity will use Discovery Learning. Have students figure the annual percentage rate of payday loans. Next, have them calculate how much is paid in a year if the person borrows against every payday. Have loan terms from local banks on hand and instruct the students to compare the costs of the two loan providers.

Debrief:

Have the students make bumper stickers about borrowing money.

Metaphor:

Borrowing money is like smoking: You know it's a bad habit, but you don't realize how bad until the cancer (debt) shows up.

■ THE FIVE-PART MODEL FOR LESSON PLAN

Language Arts: Writing

Topic:

Keeping to the topic

Engager:

Play Two Truths and a Lie.

Frame:

One of the most common problems with writing is straying from the topic. It's important to stay on the topic so the point you are trying to communicate is conveyed.

Activity:

Have the students go back to the truths they wrote in the game they played for the Engager. They will choose one of these to write about. Next, give the students each a paper with five boxes. Each of these boxes will represent a portion of the five-paragraph essay. Have the students draw in each of the boxes a cartoon of what took place. When they write, they will be describing the action in the boxes.

Debrief:

Play Give Them the Finger to ascertain whether the students understand how to stay on topic.

Metaphor:

Writing is like driving on a long-distance trip: You have to keep the destination in mind at all times. If you allow yourself to get sidetracked, you may never be able to reach the right conclusion.

THE FIVE-PART MODEL FOR LESSON PLAN ■

Math

Topic:

Making tables

Engager:

Play Quick Draw.

Frame:

Buying complicated equipment is difficult and confusing. One way to reduce the confusion is to lay the options you want side by side in tables.

Activity:

After explaining the making of tables, divide the students into pairs and have them choose a product to investigate. The product should be something that is both high-ticket and complicated. Have them list all of the options of the product that would be important to them. Next, have them find ads for these items, in newspapers or on the Internet. Have them make tables for their item, delineating the price and whether the brand has the option or not.

Debrief:

The students will play Interview the Expert and find out about each other's products. The interviewee will be able to answer questions based on the table just made.

Metaphor:

Laying information out in tables is like buying watermelon: They all look the same from the outside; you have to cut them up to see the differences.

■ THE FIVE-PART MODEL FOR LESSON PLAN

History

Topic:

The Revolutionary War

Engager:

Play Lifeboat and have the students anticipate what would be needed to spend a winter in America's northeast during the mid-eighteenth century.

Frame:

We enjoy freedom today because people were willing to pay a dear price for it. To never take it for granted, we should recognize what was done for us.

Activity:

After having studied the events of and reasons for the Revolutionary War, have students role-play both the British and the Americans, portraying their views of the war and the reasons for the war. Divide the class into two groups and have each group represent a side.

Debrief:

Have the students do a compare-and-contrast graphic organizer for the reasons for the war from both perspectives.

Metaphor:

Politics and countries are made of people. Like people, if they talked more, perhaps they could fight less.

THE FIVE-PART MODEL FOR LESSON PLAN   ■

Topic:

_____
_____
_____
_____
_____
_____

Engager:

_____
_____
_____
_____
_____
_____

Frame:

_____
_____
_____
_____
_____

Activity:

_____
_____
_____
_____
_____
_____

Debrief:

_____
_____
_____
_____
_____

Metaphor:

_____
_____
_____
_____
_____

Appendix B

Elements of Activities

1. Accessing prior knowledge: The process of reminding the students of what they already know about a topic in the effort of bridging the gap between the familiar and the unfamiliar (new).

> Transfer helps students make connections between what they already know and the new learning. It is important to remember that the connections are of value only if they are relevant to the *students'* past, not necessarily the teacher's. This process also helps the teacher find out what the students already know about the new material. If students already have knowledge of what is planned for the new lesson, then teachers should make some adjustments and move on. (Sousa, 2006, p. 150)

2. Art: The quality, production, expression, or realm, according to aesthetic principles, of what is beautiful, appealing, or of more than ordinary significance.

In his book *How the Brain Learns* (3rd ed.), David Sousa (2006) quotes Elliot Eisner of Stanford University as having identified eight cognitive competencies developed by the arts:

> The perception of relationships; an attention to nuance; the perspective that problems can have multiple solutions, and questions can have multiple answers; the ability to shift goals in process; the permission to make decisions in the absence of a rule; the use of imagination as the source of content; the acceptance of operating within constraints; and the ability to see the world from an aesthetic perspective. (pp. 215–216)

3. Building community: Building community within the classroom means making the classroom a safe place in which to learn.

> Every individual wants to be unique and to be respected for that uniqueness. Research has shown that acceptance of oneself is the first step toward filling this need. Belonging is necessary because each of us

desires to be a member of a society that appreciates us. Fitting in is more important than learning to many of our students. . . . The ability to cope and be resilient in life is very much influenced by our ability to get along with others. Our society is set up for interaction. . . . Learning is a social event; for any of us to become lifelong learners, we must engage in the process with others. (Sprenger, 2007, pp. 15–16)

4. Competition: a contest for some prize, honor, or advantage—

For a number of neural and chemical reasons, boys are more naturally aggressive and competitive than girls are. . . . the bonding chemical oxytocin greatly affects the male/female difference [with regard to competition]. With less oxytocin in the male neural and physiological system, boys tend toward greater impulsivity, more aggression, and less reliance on bonding malleability. They have less desire than girls to comply to please others, including teachers. (King & Gurian, 2006, p. 59)

5. Cooperative learning: Cooperative learning is where small teams, each with students of different levels of ability, use a variety of learning activities to improve their understanding of a subject. Each member of a team is responsible not only for learning what is taught but also for helping teammates learn, thus creating an atmosphere of achievement.

In *Classroom Instruction That Works*, Marzano, Pickering, and Pollock (2001) quote Johnson and Johnson as having identified five defining elements of cooperative learning:

The students develop a positive interdependence, they help each other learn, they have both individual and group accountability, they develop interpersonal and small group skills, and they reflect on how well the team functions together. (pp. 85–86)

6. Cross-laterals: using both right brain (global) and left brain (detail) functions—

They [the learners] can get either "left-brain stuck" or "right-brain stuck." The left side stuck is, "I've tried over and over to solve this problem, every path has been a dead end," The "right side stuck" is more overwhelming: "I'm lost—this stuff is too much." Be sure to have a "toolbox" of strategies to awaken the brain and activate both sides. In the long term, the cycles are fairly permanent. But four things can affect those highs and lows short-term: exercise, nutrition, emotions and cross laterals. (Jensen, 1997, p. 71)

7. Emotion: "Emotion is an unconscious arousal system that alerts us to potential dangers and opportunities" (Sylwester, 2005, p. 61).
"Students are much more likely to remember curriculum content in which they have made am emotional investment. For this to happen, teachers often need to use strategies that get students emotionally involved with the learning content" (Sousa, 2006, p. 84).

8. Finding patterns and making connections: The brain is a pattern-seeking device that looks for patterns in information and tries to connect new information to previously stored information.

> Since the brain already has stored patterns and structures from previous learning and experiences, teachers build on those patterns for similar information that is new. This technique makes use of the brain's search for patterns for understanding. . . . Since 80% of the learners in the classroom learn either visually or kinesthetically, it is important to include visual models to help connect the learning. (Tileston, 2005, p. 34)

9. Humor: a comic, absurd, or incongruous quality causing amusement—

In his book *How the Brain Learns* (3rd ed.), David Sousa (2006, pp. 63–64) states that there are many benefits when humor is used frequently and appropriately in the classroom. Humor gets attention, creates a positive climate, increases retention and recall, improves everyone's mental health, and provides an effective discipline tool. He suggests that humor should not be limited to an opening joke or story; rather, the teacher should look for ways to use humor within the context of the learning objective.

10. Imagination: the faculty of imagining, or of forming mental images or concepts of what is not actually present to the senses—

> When we read with comprehension, we have to create images in our minds: sights, sounds, smells, tactile sensations, muscular sensations, tastes. Reading in the content areas requires an enormous amount of intensive image making. (May, 1982, p. 413)

11. Laughter: an expression or appearance of merriment or amusement—

> Laughter provides more oxygen to the brain, causes an endorphin surge, and moderates body functions. . . . The brain runs on oxygen and glucose for fuel; laughter oxygenates the bloodstream, thereby providing more fuel for the brain. . . . Laughter causes the release into the blood of the body's natural painkillers, endorphins, which can also give the person a feeling of euphoria. . . . Finally, laughter decreases stress, muscle tension, and blood pressure. It also enhances the immune defenses. (Sousa, 2006, p. 63)

12. Making comparisons: Making comparisons refers to finding the similarities and differences among two or more things.

In *Classroom Instruction That Works*, Marzano, Pickering, and Pollock (2001) generalize that the identification of similarities and differences can be accomplished in a variety of ways. They further state that explicitly guiding the students in identifying similarities and differences, and then asking them to do it independently, enhances students' understanding of and ability to use knowledge.

13.   Making inferences: reading between the lines.

. . . when people read, they must read between the lines to understand the text. They must infer what the author didn't actually say. Such inferences are based on the reader's schemata, which in turn are based on the reader's background experiences. The teacher who ignores this basic component of the reading act cannot hope to teach reading comprehension successfully. (May, 1982, p. 122)

14.   Metacognition: awareness and understanding one's thinking and cognitive processes; thinking about thinking—

[Metacognition] is a uniquely human ability occurring in the cerebral cortex of the brain. Interestingly, it has been found that good problem solvers do it; they plan a course of action before they begin a task. They monitor themselves during the execution of the plan, they consciously back up or adjust the plan, and they evaluate themselves upon completion. (Costa, 1991, p. 11)

15.   Movement: actions or activities, as of a person or a body of persons—

Several positive things happen with more active learning. First, there's more blood flow in the body which brings more oxygen to the brain. Second, it can trigger the release of the body's "good feeling" drug, endorphin or the "challenge" hormone, adrenaline. Studies show that these are excellent for the brain. In addition, the body is often activated into states of movement which make more enthusiasm and motivation likely. And finally, activities that are learned with the body are more likely to be recalled and applied at a later date. Mind–body movement gives the body more sensory clues to be able to re-address the learning in the future. (Jensen, 1997, p. 71)

16.   Novelty: the state or quality of being new or unique—

In *Brain Compatible Strategies,* Eric Jensen (1997) says,

we all seek the stimulation that comes from novelty. The use of novelty keeps attention and interest. . . . The brain grows by novel input, not by what the students express. Novel input is what makes the brain reorganize, reallocate nerve cells to other areas and stimulate better neuronal connections. . . . In classroom learning, novel and challenging problem-solving is one way to "grow" the brain. (pp. 48–49)

17.   Problem solving: Considered the most complex of all intellectual functions, problem solving has been defined as higher-order cognitive process that requires the modulation and control of more routine or fundamental skills.

Problem solving uses sequential skills to solve complex problems and incorporates the ability to see and analyze underlying causes. These skills are necessary because students must have higher-order thinking skills in order to perform quality processes. (Tileston, 2005, p. 55)

Researchers are finding out that solving real-life problems or completing real-world projects places a learner's brain closer to the reason it exists in the first place. Therefore, information acquired when students are engaged in the strategy of project- and problem-based instruction appears to be long retained. (Tate, 2003, p. 73)

18. Question development: This is where the students develop their own questions—

The brain is more receptive to questions about new knowledge than it is to answers. Why? Curiosity is a distinct physiological state that triggers changes in our posture and eye movements and promotes chemical reactions that are advantageous to learning and recall. When we ask ourselves questions, the brain continues to process them even after they're answered. To your brain, the process is far more important than the outcome.

In short, you increase your capability of learning when you ask questions and your brain will continue to ponder the questions even after answers are found. This may explain why a laboratory or theoretical scientist remains dedicated to the pursuit of one idea for years. The quest for knowledge, not the knowledge itself, is what is so exciting. (Jensen, 2004, p. 14)

19. Rehearsal: the reprocessing of information in working memory—

The assignment of sense and meaning to new learning can occur only if the learner has adequate time to process and reprocess it. This continuing reprocessing of information is called *rehearsal,* and it is a critical component in the transference of information. . . . This type of rehearsal [rote] is used when the learner needs to remember and store information exactly as it is entered into working memory. This is not a complex strategy, but it is necessary to learn information or a cognitive skill in a specific form or sequence. (Sousa, 2006, pp. 86–87)

20. Reviewing material: the process of going over a subject again in study or recitation in order to fix it in the memory or summarize the facts—
When David Sousa (2006) refers to reviewing material, he calls it elaborative rehearsal. In his book *How the Brain Learns* (3rd ed.), he states,

This type of rehearsal is used when it is not necessary to store information exactly as learned, but when it is more important to associate the new learnings with prior learnings to detect relationships. This is a more complex thinking process in that the learner reprocesses the information several times to make connections to previous learnings and assign meaning. (p. 87)

21. Sharing opinions: expressing personal views, attitudes, or appraisals—

Association is particularly powerful when feelings or emotions are associated with a learning. We mentioned earlier that the brain's amygdala encodes emotional messages when they are strong and bonds them to learnings for long-term storage. We also noted that emotions usually have a higher priority than cognitive processing for commanding our attention. Words like *abortion, Holocaust,* and *capital punishment* often evoke strong feelings. . . . Thus, teachers should strive to bond positive feelings to new learnings so that students feel competent and can enjoy the process. . . . In this, the teacher links something from the learner's past that helps add sense and meaning to the new learning. It is important to select an experience that is clear, unambiguous, and closely relevant to the new learning. (Sousa, 2006, pp. 145–146)

22. Social interaction: Humans are social creatures. As such, they function better when they can bounce ideas off one another.

According to Gayle Gregory and Terence Parry (2006) in *Designing Brain-Compatible Learning,*

All people need to be able to interact well with others in order to form successful personal and professional relationships. The ability to work collaboratively with others is necessary not only for successful family life but also in the workplace. . . . The skills of team building, communication, leadership, and conflict resolution are as important to students as the subject content taught in schools. Students who learn to work well with others will have mastered one of the most essential skills for postschool success. (pp. 142, 148)

23. Summarization: The process of creating a comprehensive and usually brief abstract, recapitulation, or compendium of previously stated facts or statements—

"Brain research shows that having students summarize or paraphrase information is effective in helping move material into long-term memory" (Hunter, 2004, pp. 39–40).

24. Time limit: Giving the students a time limit during an activity encourages a sense of urgency.

Patricia Wolfe (2001), in *Brain Matters: Translating Research Into Classroom Practice,* states,

The neurochemical system that primes the body for emergency also stamps the moment in memory with extra vividness. Here's how neuroscientists explain this phenomenon. Epinephrine and norepinephrine, which are secreted by the adrenal cortex to activate the automatic responses . . . find their way back up to the temporal lobe of the brain. The action of these hormones in this area enhances memory for the event that activated the stress response. . . . anything you do that engages students' emotional and motivational interest will quite naturally involve this system and result in stronger memories of that which engaged the attention. . . . It is almost as if the brain has two memory systems: one for ordinary facts and one for those that are emotionally charged. (pp. 107–108)

25. Visuals: of or pertaining to seeing or sight—
Patricia Wolfe (2001), in her book *Brain Matters: Translating Research Into Classroom Practice*, states,

> Humans are intensely visual animals. The eyes contain nearly 70 percent of the body's sensory receptors and send millions of signals every second along the optic nerves to the visual processing centers of the brain. It is not surprising that the visual components of a memory are so robust. Although each of us has the ability to process kinesthetic and auditory information, we take in more information visually than through any of the other senses. (p. 153)

26. Vocalization: the process of putting thoughts into words—

> Involving the students in the presentation of the material is another approach that can be used with considerable success. An axiom from education states that if you want to know something well, teach it to someone else. Having students teach parts of the subject matter at hand involves them deeply in the material. . . . Engaging in the act of explanation will assist them in understanding it for themselves. . . . Even simple group conversation about the material will involve the students and help them remember the material at a deeper level. (Allen, 2002, p. 204)

27. Wait time: Wait time refers to the five seconds or more between the time the teacher asks a question and when he calls on a student to answer.
According to Madeline Hunter (2004) in *Mastery Teaching*,

> When we beam the question to the group and then use wait time, two things happen. First, the number of students trying to think of the answer increases, Second, the quality of the answers improves, assuming that the answer requires more than recall. (p. 17)

28. Writing: to express or communicate in written form—
In her book, *Brain Matters: Translating Research Into Classroom Practice*, Patricia Wolfe (2001) states,

> Writing and thinking are strongly linked: Writing can serve as a tool for refining thinking. At the same time, complex, cognitive activity produces more articulate and expressive writing. Writing activities fit in the category of elaborative rehearsal because they challenge students to clarify, organize, and express what they are learning. (p. 171)

References

Allen, R. (2002). *Impact teaching.* Boston: Allyn & Bacon.

Allen, R., & Kelly, D. (2004). *Let's put theory into practice.* Presented at Learning Brain Expo Conference Resources, San Diego, CA. www.impactlearn.com.

Bailey, B. (1998). *Brain smart teaching & living.* Unpublished manuscript, University of Central Florida, Orlando, Florida.

Bevill, K. (2004). *Learning in motion: Why the brain needs movement.* Presented at Learning Brain Expo Conference Resources, San Diego, CA. www.impactlearn.com.

Campbell, L., Campbell, B., & Dickinson, D. (2004). *Teaching and learning through multiple intelligences* (3rd ed.) Boston: Pearson Education.

Costa, A. L. (1991). *The school as a home for the mind.* Thousand Oaks, CA: Corwin Press.

Gardner, H. (1983). *Frames of mind: The theory of multiple intelligences.* New York: Basic Books.

Gregory, G., & Parry, T. (2006). *Designing brain-compatible learning.* Thousand Oaks, CA: Corwin Press.

Hunter, R. (2004). *Madeline Hunter's mastery teaching: Increasing instructional effectiveness in elementary and secondary schools.* Thousand Oaks, CA: Corwin Press.

Jensen, E. (1997). *Brain compatible strategies.* Thousand Oaks, CA: Corwin Press.

Jensen, E. (2007). *Introduction to Brain-Compatible Learning,* 2nd ed. Thousand Oaks, CA. Corwin Press.

Kagan, S., & Kagan, M. (1998). *Multiple intelligences: The complete MI Book.* San Clemente, CA: Kagan Cooperative Learning.

Kagan Cooperative Learning. (2001). *SmartCards.* San Clemente, CA: Author.

King, K., & Gurian, M. (2006, September). The brain—his and hers. *Educational Leadership, 64* (1), 59.

Markowitz, K., & Jensen, E. (1999). *The great memory book.* Thousand Oaks, CA: Corwin Press.

Marzano, R., Pickering, D., & Pollock, J. (2001). *Classroom instruction that works.* Alexandria, VA: Association for Supervision and Curriculum Development.

May, F. (1982). *Reading as communication.* Toronto, Ontario Canada: Merrill Publishing Company.

Payne, R. (2001). *Learning structures.* Highland, TX: aha! Process.

Sousa, D. (2006). *How the brain learns* (3rd ed.). Thousand Oaks, CA: Corwin Press.

Sprenger, M. (2007). *Becoming a "wiz" at brain-based teaching* (2nd ed.). Thousand Oaks, CA: Corwin Press.

Summers, H. B. (2006). *Debate.* Retrieved September 23, 2006, from http://ftp.ev1 .net/%7Earcwynd/debate/debate.htm

Sylwester, R. (2005). *How to explain a brain.* Thousand Oaks, CA: Corwin Press.

Tate, M. (2003). *Worksheets don't grow dendrites.* Thousand Oaks, CA: Corwin Press.

Tileston, D. (2005). *10 best teaching practices.* Thousand Oaks, CA: Corwin Press.

Wiggins, G., & McTighe, J. (1998). *Understanding by design: Professional developmental workbook..* Alexandria, VA: Association for Supervision and Curriculum Development.

Wolfe, P. (2001). *Brain matters: Translating research into classroom practice.* Alexandria, VA: Association for Supervision and Curriculum Development.

Index